GOD'S LOST CAUSE

A Study of the Church and the Racial Problem

DATE DUE

Demco, Inc. 38-293

JEAN RUSSELL

GOD'S

A STUDY OF THE CHURCH

LOST

AND THE RACIAL PROBLEM

CAUSE

THE JUDSON PRESS
VALLEY FORGE

Standard Book Number 8170-0458-0

Library of Congress Catalog Card Number 78-82155

First printing 1969

© SCM Press Ltd 1968

Printed in Great Britain

CONTENTS

All attempts to interpret the past are indirect attempts to understand the present and its future. Men try to remember the road they have travelled in order that they may gain some knowledge of the direction in which it is leading, for their stories are begun without prevenient knowledge of the end. They are always on their way before they know where they are going and they are impelled to travel by motives other than a sure anticipation of the goal.

. . . Yet the sailor who seeks to find his bearings by consulting the charts his fathers used when they set out on the voyage he is continuing, by noting all the corrections they have made upon them and by looking for the stars which gave them orientation may claim at least that he is trying to be true to the meaning of the voyage.

H. Richard Niebuhr

INTRODUCTION

In January of 1961 a small group of Negro and white students were sprawled on the floor of my lounge drinking coffee and discussing their plans for the future of the Student Movement. They were on their way to Georgia for a meeting of SNCC,[1] and my home in Tennessee had over the previous six years become a half-way house where Negroes and whites travelling together from north to south could rest before advancing farther into 'enemy territory'. The students were relaxed and yet exhilarated. In one year with their sit-in movement they had begun to knock down walls which had barely been cracked by legislation. Theirs were the faces which had remained calm and impassive as mobs of white juveniles and adults cursed, jeered, spat upon them, and forcibly tore them from the stools of lunch counters across the South. These were the young people who had done their time in jail for disturbing the peace – the boys packed into cells with white vagrants and hardened criminals, the girls with prostitutes, shoplifters, and alcoholics – and who had disturbed the peace of the jails by their persistent voicing of their theme song, *We Shall Overcome*. These were university students who had put down their textbooks and had taken up a cause. Their credo was non-violence, and they had remained true to it in the face of the unbelievable violence of angry, hysterical white mobs and sullen, hostile white policemen backed up by fire hoses and murderous police dogs. Theirs were the beautiful faces in the south in 1961.

[1] Student Non-Violent Co-ordinating Committee, which will be discussed in detail at a later point.

The desultory conversation began to focus on their plans for the SNCC meeting. A matter high on their agenda was a decision as to how they would celebrate their first anniversary. It was agreed that there must be a most dramatic and united attack on some bastion of segregation, and that the kick-off day should be February 1, the day on which in 1960 the sit-in movement was launched by four Negro students at a lunch counter in Greensboro, North Carolina. The students in my home discussed with some emotion but with realism various segregated facilities and institutions. There were schools, public libraries, public recreational facilities, public accommodations – and then someone said, 'The churches, of course.' I said I thought that this might be a good time to make some move in that direction. A student picked it up and said, 'We could do kneel-ins or pray-ins.' There were a few scattered giggles and then silence. I said 'Why not?' And this time there was a longer silence and one could sense a bit of embarrassment because these students knew that my own involvement had a religious orientation. Finally, one of the students said with no hostility – in fact with no emotion at all unless it were boredom – 'The churches! Oh, God, Jean, who wants them?'

Three years later Benjamin Mays, president of a Negro college and a respected Negro leader in the Christian community, predicted that churches in the United States would eventually become desegregated 'because in time all other agencies in the community will have been desegregated . . . and the church will have to follow in order to save face, to catch up with the procession.'[2]

The charge which is brought against American Protestantism is not only that it has failed in this crisis period in race relations to make a witness to the unity of mankind, but that its historical record could not lead one to expect such a witness. This has been especially true of the Negro community's evaluation of the white Christian community, but it has also been true of the analysis offered by historians, sociologists, and economists regardless of colour. All have recorded in their discussion of racial

[2] Benjamin E. Mays, 'The Churches Will Follow', *The Christian Century*, April 22, 1964, p. 513.

problems in the United States that over the centuries Protestant churches have played an almost negligible role in the struggle of the Negro towards legal and social acceptance. One writer has put it even more strongly: 'For years, most of our churches have aided and abetted the Anglo-Saxon white conspiracy.'[3]

With very few exceptions writers have attributed the churches' impotence in race relations to those same factors which are used to explain the general inability of the United States to deal with its colour problem. These are of an economic, political, or sociological nature, and the church has been seen as one institution among institutions which is responsive to these factors. If one accepts this thesis in its entirety, one can only conclude that there is no relationship between the theology of American churches and their social ethics. Although it is possible that the role of theology has been to provide a rationalization of attitudes based on prejudice, economic conditions, and social factors, it is equally possible that the ethical failure of Protestantism stems from its theological failure.

This latter possibility cannot but have occurred to those persons who have found themselves involved in the civil rights struggle as a result of their allegiance to the Christian community. There may be any number of reasons why such a thesis has not been explored. It is true that the diversity of American Protestantism makes the search for any pattern a formidable one.[4] However, as one looks at this history, one is struck by the fact that there are movements within it which have had a pervasive influence on all denominational theology and which have not been confined to a single historical period. Three movements – Puritanism, revivalism, and the Social Gospel movement – have not only been decisive in shaping the past but seem to continue to mould the present. None of these

[3] Robert Spike, 'Our Churches' Sin Against the Negro', Reprint, *Look*, May 18, 1965.

[4] Estimates of the number of denominations in the United States range from 200 (Henry Steele Commager, *The American Mind*, New Haven, Yale University Press, 1950, p. 184) to more than 400 (Elmer T. Clark, *The Small Sects in America*, Nashville, The Abingdon Press, 1959).

movements is unique to the American scene, so it cannot be
contended that they were conditioned primarily by American
culture. Therefore, it would seem possible that by looking at the
theology of these three movements, the actual racial situation
during the periods when these movements were dominant,
and the witness of the churches during these periods, one might
find in the past some illumination for the difficult path of the
future.

But at the present time to devote adequate time to an investigation of the historical relationship between the theology of
American Protestantism and its posture in the area of race
relations is to lay oneself open to the accusation of withdrawing
from the battlefield while the war is being waged and when its
outcome is still undetermined. And why would one leave the
battlefield in the midst of the battle? After all, the churches
have long been accused of inaction, and it was only in the mid-
1960's that churches as national institutions began to take an
active role in the civil rights struggle. This is not to say that
Christians have been totally uninvolved. As early as 1640 Roger
Williams concerned himself with the property rights of American Indians and with their inclusion in the church.[5] The anti-
slavery crusade was for a period of time almost solely in the
hands of the clergy and Quakers. In the 1920's much of organized Christianity was on record as being opposed to the terrorism
and lynching to which the Negro had been subjected throughout the twentieth century. But the 1960's have been the churches'
shining hour. For one of the few times in its history the religious
community has been given credit for having been the decisive
influence in the passage of important social legislation, the Civil
Rights Act of 1964.[6] One would withdraw from this battle only
because of a strong concern as to whether action in and of itself
constitutes faithful witness. Even those who are most impatient
with the impotency of the churches suggest that only that
activity which is consistent with the being of the churches is apt

[5] William Haller, *Liberty and Reformation in the Puritan Revolution* (New
York, Columbia University Press, 1955), pp. 154-155.
[6] *Reports*, The Commission on Religion and Race (The National Council of
Churches of Christ in the U.S.A.), Vol. 1, No. 1.

to be sustained.[7] The churches' self-understanding must dictate their involvement in the world. This is to say that if the Church does not rightly understand itself it will not rightly understand the world, and its involvement with the world will be a sporadic and superficial attempt at 'problem-solving'. There is strong evidence that the all-out effort in civil rights which was made by the Protestant churches in the 1960's was of this nature, and historical investigation indicates that such has been generally true of its involvement with social issues. It is, therefore, an appropriate time to examine the thesis that there may be within the theology of American Protestantism a fatal weakness which may account for its ethical failure.

It has only been seen clearly for the past three or four years that prejudice and discrimination against the American Negro are not confined to the southern states. The 'long, hot summers' have become longer and hotter in the ghettoes of northern and western cities than in the south. Watts, Harlem, and Newark have presented the world with as ugly pictures of rioting, violence, and brutality as did Birmingham, Jackson, and New Orleans. That this has happened is a matter for deep regret, but it has freed the student of race relations from the burden of attempting to discover in one specific historical situation the basis of prejudice. It should now be clear to the reasonably observant that racial prejudice exists (even if quiescent) in the majority of people – and that in the proper conditions and with the proper combination of social, economic, and political factors, any town and any country may be ripped open by its ugliness.

During the time I have lived in Scotland, a number of events have occurred which have led me to believe that Great Britain has a colour problem of an intensity and magnitude which she may not yet have understood. There was the notorious Smeth-

7 'The clergy and many white people are, for the first time, going into overt action on behalf of an eternal principle which they presumably believed and preached all the time. In this case, conscience seems to have been aroused only after the movement, initiated and led by the injured party, gained momentum and showed some signs of success . . . White people, including the moral and religious functionaries, may persist only so long as they are restless and need a cause. Perhaps some other cause will win them away. Or perhaps they will lose their taste for causes.' Everett C. Hughes, 'Race Relations and the Sociological Imagination', *Race*, Vol. V, No. 3, January 1964, pp. 15-16.

wick political campaign, and the candidate won that election
with as bigoted and intemperate campaign speeches as a Tal-
madge of Georgia or a Wallace of Alabama. The formation of a
Race Relations Board has been met with the same superficial
criticism which has been made of the attempts of the United
States government to combat discrimination – 'You can't legis-
late morality'. The newspapers contain letters from well-mean-
ing citizens who during a time of economic difficulty and
unemployment express the view that coloured persons should
be returned to their own countries in order that there be more
job opportunities for 'our own people'.

But my most striking impressions have been obtained at a
personal level as I have talked with University, SCM, YWCA,
and public school groups on the subject of race relations. During
the question or discussion period, one of the questions always
asked me has been, 'But what do you think of intermarriage?'
My personal view as a Christian that marriage is a covenant
between two persons in the presence of and under the judgment
of God and that therefore the question is relevant only in
a specific situation is as widely rejected in this country as it was
in the United States.

The first year I lived in Edinburgh I attended a conference
sponsored by the University of Edinburgh. Half the participants
were Scottish students, and half were overseas students of
African and Indian descent. The conference was well devised in
that race relations was not on the agenda and only came to the
surface as the result of the confrontation between racial groups.
But come to the surface it did, and as I sat listening to those
students, I could have closed my eyes and been at the earliest
student conferences I attended in the United States. There was
the same 'talking at' and inability to hear which seems always
to characterize early attempts at communication between
students of different racial groups. There was the almost desperate groping for understanding by a few seriously committed
young white students who generally ended up telling their personal experiences and being reduced to tears. There was the in-
sensitive calloused parroting of clichés by other white students –
'But you want to live with your own kind, don't you?' – when

the problem of University housing for coloured students was discussed. There was the final proud, cold aloofness and withdrawal by African students who were sons and daughters of chiefs and heads of states and who were being spoken to condescendingly and patronizingly by the sons and daughters of shopkeepers and miners. And there was the unanimous rejection of the one student who timidly mentioned Christianity.

As I listened, I thought of January 1961 and the students on my lounge floor who had made their painful way through confrontation with each other and were therefore able for a time to confront together a largely hostile society. But the difficulty and fragility of the relationship they had established has become apparent now as SNCC has become the platform for the Black Power leaders who view with increasing condescension earlier inter-racial efforts. *We Shall Overcome* has been replaced by the battle cry, 'Burn, baby, burn'.

In the face of the facts I continue to believe that there is a significant role for the Church in the confusion and chaos of this 20th-century racial confrontation. It is this belief which has led to the study upon which this book is based.[8]

---

[8] This belief is only reinforced by the increasingly tragic chain of events in the United States. When this manuscript was sent to my publisher in April, I was in the United States when Dr Martin Luther King was assassinated. I returned to Scotland and received the book in proof form. Today as I was completing the proof reading, I have listened to the news reports concerning the assassination of Senator Robert Kennedy. The guilt for the murder of these men who advocated justice for all men cannot be placed neatly or easily on the shoulders of certain assassins. All of us share equally in the inhumanity or humanity of the world.

I

PURITANISM AND
THE NEGRO

Historians disagree as to when the Negro's tortured existence in the United States began. The statistics and records for the Colonial period are unreliable – perhaps because the colonists were too busily engaged in subduing Indians and their new wild environment to keep accurate count of very many things. Historians date the introduction of slavery into the Colonies between the years of 1619 and 1650. Evidence would seem to favour the theory that the first slaves arrived on the ship *Desire* in 1638.[1]

The enslavement of American Indians was accepted as a matter of course by most colonists. Unfortunately for the African forebears of American Negroes, the American Indian made a very poor slave indeed. He either sickened and died in captivity, or his superior knowledge of his untamed homeland enabled him to escape in which case he inevitably took a few scalps home with him. It finally occurred to the inventive Puritan mind that there was a more profitable way to dispose of the Indian problem. In a letter written in 1645 to John Winthrop, governor of the Massachusetts Bay Colony, a citizen by the name of Emmanuel (which is to say, 'God with us') Downing made the following proposal:

A war with the Narragansett is very considerable to this plantation, for I doubt whether it be not sin in us, having power in our hands, to suffer them to maintain the worship of the devil which

[1] Lorenzo J. Greene, *The Negro in Colonial New England* (New York, Columbia University Press, 1942), p. 17.

their paw waws often do. Secondly, if upon a just war the Lord should deliver them into our hands, we might easily have men, women, and children enough to exchange for Moors, which will be more gainful pillage for us than we conceive, for I do not see how we can thrive until we get into a stock of slaves . . .[2]

This suggestion seems to have been adopted, and many Indians who were taken captive were used to barter for African slaves. One can only surmise that those Indians who lived through a voyage by slave ship and found themselves in a strange land became more tractable and therefore worthy to be exchanged for Africans.

The first American slave ship, the *Desire*, sailed from Marblehead Massachusetts, in 1636. The famous triangular route between New England, the African coast, and the West Indies was travelled by ships whose cargoes consisted of rum, sugar, and slaves. Originally the slaves were sold to sugar growers in the Islands, but gradually more and more went to the English Colonies on the mainland. The accounts of the misery, suffering, and terror of the Africans who were chained together in the holds of slave ships – for a voyage which only the strongest survived and these broken in heart, body, and spirit – make for very unpleasant reading. However, the most respected of New England citizens invested in the early slave voyages. The editor of Governor Winthrop's *Journals* comments that slave trading was taken as the ordinary course of business by a man of Winthrop's generation.[3]

But the mortality rate on the slave vessels was very high, and the number of Negro slaves in the Colonies was limited until the 18th century. Governor Dudley of Massachusetts reported only 550 Negroes in that Colony in 1708.[4] It is also true that slavery did not flourish in the New England Colonies as it did in the southern Colonies because the climate of the north was unfavourable for the health of the slaves. Those who remained

---

[2] Quoted in Louis B. Wright, *The Colonial Civilisation of North America 1607-1763*, (London, Eyre & Spottiswoode, 1949), pp. 91-92.

[3] John Winthrop, *Journal, History of New England, 1630-1649*, Editor, James K. Hosmer, Vol. I (New York, Barnes & Noble Inc., 1959), p. 227.

[4] James Truslow Adams, *The American* (New York, Charles Scribner's Sons, 1943), p. 125.

were utilized as domestic servants, because the principal need was for skilled labour which the African slave could not provide. Even so, the figure rose from the 550 slaves reported in Massachusetts in 1708 to 2,000 in 1715 and to approximately 6,000 in 1776.[5]

We shall examine the slave system in New England and specifically in the Massachusetts Bay Colony because it was there that Puritanism in its most unadulterated form existed, and this should enable us to see more clearly the relationship between the theology and ethics of the movement. The Puritans who settled the Massachusetts Bay Colony were not driven from England but left of their own accord and for their own purposes. That their motivations were mixed is undoubtedly true. This group of Puritans saw their task as being that of completing the Reformation, and they believed that in a new land they would establish a Colony of God which would be a model for all Christendom. Their belief was attested by the lay sermon preached by John Winthrop aboard the *Arabella* on the voyage to the new land in which he said:

. . . when hee shall make us a prayse and glory, that men shall say of succeeding plantacions: the Lord make it like that of New England: for wee must consider that wee shall be as a citty upon a Hill, the eies of people are uppon us . . .[6]

The eyes of all people could see that the establishment of a thriving industry based on the sale of human beings was not generally repugnant to the Puritan conscience. Nor was the ownership of those human beings. Slaves were owned by such noted New England divines as John Cotton, Cotton Mather, Ezra Stiles, John Davenport, and Jonathan Edwards. Individual voices were raised against the institution of slavery, but let us look first at the general situation.

The earliest recorded legalization of slavery in the Colonies was that of the first legal code of Massachusetts, the Body of Liberties of 1641, which prohibited 'bond-slavery' for the inhabitants of the Colony but permitted enslavement of those 'who

[5] Greene, *op. cit.*, appendix.
[6] H. Shelton Smith; Robert T. Handy; Lefferts A. Loetscher, *American Christianity*, Vol. I (New York, Charles Scribner's Sons, 1960), p. 102.

are sold to us'. Specific legislation dealing with the treatment
of slaves did not begin to appear until the latter decades of the
17th century. Massachusetts adopted legislation prohibiting
marriage between whites and Negroes; prohibiting sexual relations between Negroes and Englishmen; imposing a 9 p.m.
curfew on Negroes and Indians; requiring the posting of bond
by a slave-owner who wished to free a slave; and imposing the
punishment of severe whipping on any Negro striking an
Englishman or a member of 'another Christian nation'.[7]

The slave system was an enigma in that slaves were seen under
the law as both property and persons. They were taxable to their
owners as property – in fact, in the category of domestic animals.
However, as persons they had the right to their lives, rights in
court, the right to serve in the armed forces, and the right to
hold property. The marriage laws were the same for slaves and
whites, and after that time when ministers were allowed to perform the marriage ceremony, many illustrious Puritan ministers
performed the ceremony for slaves. As early as 1692 a slave
named Candy discovered that she had the right to be tried
for witchcraft. She was acquitted, but the fate of another slave
jailed on the same charge remains unknown.[8]

The question of the right to vote was complicated by the relationship which existed between the church and the civil community. In the years between 1631 and 1664 the right to vote
was dependent upon church membership. There is evidence
that slaves became members of churches, but there is no evidence that a Negro was ever considered a member of the Company of the Massachusetts Bay. Had this happened it would have
been possible for a slave (a chattel) who was a church member
to have been involved in passing legislation binding upon his
master who might have been a non-church member. There is no
record of Negroes voting at any time in Colonial New England
which would indicate that even free Negroes were disenfran-
chised.[9]

---

[7] Carl N. Degler, 'Slavery and the Genesis of American Race Prejudice',
Comparative Studies in Society and History, Vol. II, No. 1, October 1959,
pp. 62-63.
[8] Greene, *op. cit.*, pp. 153-177.
[9] *Ibid.*, p. 262.

B

While it is quite clear that there was no general protest against slavery, individual voices were raised against it. The most notorious of these was that of Judge Samuel Sewall who has been characterized as a 'learned, pious, and honoured magistrate' who 'entered the lists alone, and sounded his solitary blast in the ears of his brother magistrates and the people, who listened in amazement and wonder, not unmingled with sorrow and contempt'.[10] Sewall was himself a trader in slaves and a slaveholder. In both political and ecclesiastical affairs he was usually to be identified with the more conservative elements of the community. He had sat on the bench for the Salem witch trials and had five years thereafter publicly confessed his sense of guilt concerning those trials. Four years later he issued his anti-slavery manifesto which he entitled 'The Selling of Joseph'.[11] There is no record of his having been prompted to write the pamphlet by any event other than the stirring of his own conscience.

Sewall's utilization and understanding of the Old and New Testaments combined with his enlightened approach towards the social practices of his day concerning Negroes resulted in a document which is very nearly *sui generis* in the story of American slavery. It is also significant in that the pro-slavery arguments which Sewall refuted are largely Scriptural, so that though one finds little record of these arguments among Puritan writings, one can assume that they were in rather wide circulation. Let us look at these arguments and Sewall's handling of them:

(1) *These Blackamores are of the Posterity of Cham, and therefore under the Curse of Slavery*. Gen. 9.25, 26, 27. Sewall replied that one would not choose to be an 'Executioner of the Vindicative Wrath of God; the extent and duration of which is to us uncertain'. He also said that it was Canaan who was cursed and not Cham, and that the Blackamores were not descendents of Canaan but of Cush, and that Ovid was probably right in attri-

---

[10] George H. Moore, *Notes on the History of Slavery in Massachusetts* (New York, D. Appleton & Co., 1866), pp. 81-82.

[11] Samuel Sewall, 'The Selling of Joseph', *American Issues*, Vol. I, Editors, W. Thorp; M. E. Curti; C. H. Baker (Chicago, J. B. Lippincott Company, 1944), pp. 65-67.

buting their colour to the extreme heat of Ethiopia which drew
their blood to the surface of their bodies.

(2) *The Nigers are brought out of a Pagan Country, into
place where the Gospel is preached.* Sewall responded that evil
must not be done that good may come of it.

(3) *The Africans have Wars one with another: Our ships bring
lawful Captives taken in those Wars.* Sewall's answer was that
all wars are unjust on one side, and since they had no way to
know which was the just side, they could not know if the captives were lawful. Furthermore, *'Therefore all things whatsoever
ye would that men should do to you, do ye so to them.'*

(4) *Abraham had servants bought with his Money, and born
in his House.* And here Sewall's logic reaches its climax. 'Until
the Circumstances of *Abraham's* purchase be recorded, no Argument can be drawn from it.'[12]

Sewall's conclusion deserves quotation in full:

And since the partition Wall is broken down, inordinate Self love
should likewise be demolished. GOD expects that Christians should
be of a more Ingenuous and benign frame of spirit. Christians should
carry it to all the World, as the Israelites were to carry it one
towards another. And for men obstinately to persist in holding their
Neighbours and Brethren under the Rigor of perpetual Bondage,
seems to be no proper way of gaining Assurance that God has given
them Spiritual Freedom. Our Blessed Saviour has altered the Measures of the ancient Love-Song, and set it to a most excellent New
Tune, which all ought to be ambitious of Learning. Matt. 5.43, 44.
John 13.34. These Ethopians, as black as they are: seeing they are
the Sons and Daughters of the First *Adam*, the Brethren and
Sisters of the Last ADAM, and the offspring of GOD, They ought
to be treated with a Respect agreeable.[13]

Judge Sewall's treatise did not go unanswered. In 1701 John
Saffin replied with 'A Brief and Candid Answer to a late Printed
Sheet, entitled, The Selling of Joseph'. Saffin was not a man of
the stature of Sewall in the community, but he was a prominent
jurist, merchant, and slave trader. He was involved in a problem
with one of his own slaves which may have accounted for the
alacrity of his responses to Sewall. He had promised a slave
his freedom and then had bound him over to another man. The

[12] *Ibid.*, pp. 65-66.   [13] *Ibid.*, p. 67.

slave sued Saffin in 1701, and the court (of which Sewall was a
member) ruled against Saffin in 1703.[14]

Saffin's defence of slavery was made in the light of his understanding of the doctrine of election. He wrote with none of
Sewall's admirable clarity and terseness, so he can only be
quoted:

> . . . True, but what is all this to the purpose, to prove that all
> men have equal rights to Liberty, and all outward comforts of this
> life; which Position seems to invert the order that God hath set in
> the World, who hath ordained different degrees and orders of men,
> some to be High and Honourable, some to be low and Despicable;
> some to be Monarchs, . . . Masters, . . . others to be subjects, and
> to be Commanded; Servants of sundry sorts and degrees, bound to
> obey, yea some to be born Slaves, and so to remain during their
> lives, as hath been proved. Otherwise there would be a mere parity
> among men, contrary to that of the Apostle, *I Cor. 12 from the 13
> to the 26 verse*, where he sets forth (by way of comparison) the differ-
> ent sorts and offices of the Members of the Body, indigitating that
> they are all of use, but not equal, and of like dignity. So God hath
> set different Orders and Degrees of men in the World, both in
> Church and Common Weal. Now, if this Position of parity should
> be true, it would then follow that the ordinary course of Divine
> Providence of God in the World should be wrong and unjust, (which
> we must not dare to think, much less to affirm) and all the sacred
> Rules, Precepts, and Commands of the Almighty which he hath
> given the Sons of Men to observe and keep in their respective Places,
> Orders and Degrees, would be to no purpose; which unaccount-
> ability derogates from the Divine Wisdom of the most High, who
> hath made nothing in vain, but hath Holy Ends in all his Dispensa-
> tions to the Children of men.[15]

The documents of Sewall and Saffin are among the few preserved which record the fact that slavery was to any extent a
controversial issue in the Colonial period.

Documentation concerning the Puritan attitude towards the
evangelization and conversion of slaves is also limited. England's attitude towards conversion was favourable. In 1660 instructions were given by the King to the Council for Foreign
Plantations, one of which was:

---

[14] Greene, *op. cit.*, p. 183.
[15] William Sumner Jenkins, *Pro-Slavery Thought in the Old South* (Chapel
Hill, University of North Carolina Press, 1935), pp. 5-6.

And you are to consider how such of the Natives or such as are purchased by you from other parts to be servants or slaves may be best invited to the Christian Faith, and be made capable of being baptized thereunto, it being to the honor of our Crowne and of the Protestant Religion that all persons in any of our Dominions should be taught the knowledge of God, and be made acquainted with the ministries of Salvation.[16]

Instructions to governors of the Colonies often contained a clause urging them to use their efforts to accelerate the conversion of slaves. However, the Massachusetts Bay Colony was so nearly self-governed in its early years as to accept little in the way of instructions or suggestions from England.

The idea was prevalent in the American colonies that under English law a baptized slave might claim his freedom. This placed conscientious masters in a dilemma: to deny baptism to their slaves would retard the missionary enterprise (and damn souls in the event that slaves possessed souls); to allow baptism might result in the loss of their property. To get around this problem a number of Colonies passed acts specifically denying that baptism was a cause for manumission. A group of ministers in Massachusetts requested such an act in a memorial to the General Court in 1694 stating that masters denied their slaves the privilege of baptism, but no act was passed.[17]

One of the most extensive records of an individual Puritan concern is found in Cotton Mather's diary. In October 1717 there is an entry: 'A strange Providence of GOD, has brought into my Family a new Servant; a Negro boy of promising circumstances. Oh! Lett me use all possible Projections and Endeavours, to make him a Servant of the Lord. That this may be kept in Mind, I call him, Obadiah.'[18] The 'strange Providence' to which Mather referred was that the Negro was purchased for him by his church congregation.

In 1723 Mather wrote to the Reverend Thomas Prince concerning a Negro who was to be executed for having burned a

[16] Marcus W. Jernegan, 'Slavery and Conversion in the American Colonies', *American Historical Review*, Vol. 21, No. 3, April 1916, p. 514.
[17] *Ibid.*
[18] Cotton Mather, *The Diary of Cotton Mather* (Boston, Massachusetts Historical Society Collections, 2 Vols., 1911-1912), p. 477.

white man's house. There were rumours of a servile insurrection
to burn the town. Prince was evidently preparing a lecture and
Mather sent him suggestions for the lecture based on the subject
of the threatened burning of the town. In part he said:

And Considering by what Hands the Town has been so Endangered, there can be nothing more seasonable and reasonable
than for us, to Consider whether our Conduct with relation to our
African Slaves, be not one thing for which our God may have a
Controversy with us.

Are they always treated according to the Rules of Humanity?

And much more, Christianity which is improved and Ennobled
Humanity.

Are they treated as those, that are of one Blood with us, and those
that have Immortal Souls in them, and are not meer Beasts of
Burden?

Are they instructed and made to know?

Such things, which if they knew, would restrain them from
Exorbitancies and Enormities which are Complained (against) them,
and render them notable Blessings in the Families they belong unto.

The Common Cavil, that they are the worse servants, for being
taught the Knowledge of CHRIST, is a Cursed Falshood; Experience
confutes it; It is a Blasphemy; and it is fitter for the Mouth of a
Devil, than of a Christian, to utter it.

But then, there is a Voice of Heaven, to the Slaves, on what this
poor Creature is Left unto.

To Beware of the Sins, which may provoke the glorious one to
Leave them unto the Last Degrees of Wickedness and Misery.

To study a Dutiful Behaviour unto their Superiours; and that they
may be blessings in the Family they belong unto.

To be patient in their Low and hard Conditions.

To become the Servants of CHRIST.

Then, what they shall very shortly see, at the End of their Short
Servitude.

Else a worse thing.[19]

We do not know if Prince followed Mather's suggestions as
to his lecture. Mather does not indicate in his diary what success
he had in converting slaves. Religious instruction for slaves
was certainly a concern of his, and he opened a short-lived school
for Negroes and Indians.[20] There is an entry in his diary which
reads: 'I have a Number of black Sheep in my Flock, which

[19] *Ibid.*, pp. 687-688.   [20] Greene, *op. cit.*, p. 238.

it is time for me again, to send for; and pray with them, and preach to them, and enquire into their Conduct, and encourage them, in the ways of Piety: A Religious Society of Negroes.'[21]

Any precise determination of a general Puritan attitude towards the baptism and full church membership of slaves is complicated by the fact that each congregation had local autonomy. There is evidence that some slaves were baptized and became church members, but the preponderance of evidence indicates that this was a limited number who were not allowed a vote in church affairs and who were segregated in the congregations as well as in their graveyards.[22]

The inevitable question is how it could be that a people with one of the strongest senses of divine mission since the Old Testament period and who possessed an intricately constructed theology and elaborately devised moral code could enslave members of their own species and in most instances refuse to baptize those 'heathen'. To determine if any clue to this enigma is to be found in the Covenant theology of the Puritans involves extensive reading in the works of both the English and New England Puritan divines, as the latter accepted the former as their mentors and models. New England Puritanism was built solidly on the foundation erected by William Perkins, William Ames, and John Preston. Perkins and Preston were Cambridge theologians, and Ames was a student of Perkins who was forced to flee to Holland to expound his theology. Most students of Puritan theology contend that New England theologians made no original contribution to the theological system. It would be out of the question to attempt to reproduce here the detailed analysis of Puritan theology which was necessary background material for this section. We shall instead confine ourselves to a fairly brief and general résumé of those results of this study which seem to cast important light on the Puritan's abortive relationship to his black brother.

Covenant Theology

The belief that God has joined himself to his people in a cove-

[21] *Ibid.*, p. 532.   [22] *Ibid.*, pp. 282-284.

nant relationship was not peculiar to the Puritans but has played
some role in all of Reformed theology. But the doctrine of the
Covenant achieved centrality in Puritanism, and it became
the normative theological concept for the ordering of all doctrine
as well as ecclesiastical, political, and social life. One of the
Puritan theologians stated it this way:

There is no ground you have to beleeve you shall be saved, there
is no ground to beleeve that any promise of God shall be made good
to you, to beleeve that you shall have the price of the high calling
of God in Jesus Christ, and those glorious riches of the inheritance
prepared for us in him: I say, there is no other ground at all, but
upon this Covenant: all that wee teach you, from day to day, are
but conclusions drawne from this Covenant, they are all built upon
this . . .[23]

The Covenant theologians believed that God had always dealt
with man in terms of covenant. The first covenant was made
with Adam, and in that covenant God promised Adam and his
posterity eternal life if Adam would obey the moral law which
was planted in his heart. Adam's failure to do so incurred for
him a just penalty. This first covenant was known as the Covenant of Works.

God then made a second covenant, this with Abraham, in
which he promised to be the God of Abraham and his children;
the condition for Abraham was simply that of faith. This was
the Covenant of Grace which was the same in both Old and
New Testament times but which differed only in ministration.
Abraham was to believe that Christ would come, and Christians
were to believe that Christ had come. Because of man's inability
to keep the moral law, God in Christ would take, or had taken,
the task upon himself; man was to believe this and live in
gratitude to his Covenant Partner.

The Covenant of Works was not abrogated by the Covenant
of Grace but was incorporated into it, in that the new law which
was the condition of the first covenant remained as the rule of
life and manners according to which persons in the Covenant

[23] John Preston, *The New Covenant, or the Saints Portion* (London, 1643),
p. 351.

of Grace should live. The law was not a condition of the covenant, but as John Cotton said, '. . . as the Law is given by
Christ, it is not a Covenant of Works, but a Commandment of
well-doing; and he having given it, we take ourselves bound to
be subject to it',[24] and 'So that the children of the Covenant of
Grace will only tell you, that they are free from the Covenant of
Law, but not from the Commandment of it . . .'[25]

In an analysis of the Federal theology of John Coccejus who
was a student of Ames and whose theology was in basic agreement with other Covenant theologians, Karl Barth (in whose
own theology the covenant concept finds a place of high importance[26]) raises the question of how 'men who knew the Scriptures
as Coccejus and his fellows undoubtedly did' could have allowed
a Covenant of Works to become the schema in which the Covenant of Grace was set up. He concludes that 'biblical exegesis
had been invaded by a mode of thought in which . . . history,
however extraordinary the course it took, could only unfold itself
and therefore only begin as the history of man and his works,
man who is good by nature and who is therefore in covenant
with God − a God who is pledged to him by virtue of his goodness'.[27]

Herein would seem to lie the crux of the matter − that the
covenant concept became the schema for man's interpretation of
his history and actions rather than a doctrine the meaning
of which lay in its value as an instrument for understanding
God's actions towards man. But let us not be too easily beguiled
by Barth's statement of the flaw of Covenant theology. Let us
look for ourselves at the way in which this ordering principle
affected the fundamental doctrines of God, man, Jesus Christ,
and the Church in Puritan theology.

[24] John Cotton, *A Treatise of the Covenant of Grace* (London, 1671), p. 74.
[25] *Ibid.*, p. 88.
[26] 'We cannot, therefore, think of Him except as the one who has concluded
and set up this covenant with us. We would be mistaking Him, we would
obviously be making ourselves guilty of transgression, of sin, if we were to
try to think of Him otherwise, if we were to try to know and fear and love
any other God but Him − the One who from the very first, from the creation
of heaven and earth, has made Himself the covenant God of man, our covenant God.' Karl Barth, *Church Dogmatics*, IV, 1 (Edinburgh, T. & T. Clark,
1956), p. 38.
[27] *Ibid.*, p. 62.

1. *Of God*

The Covenant God was incomprehensible and unknowable except in so far as he chose to make himself known. But this God
had chosen to reveal himself to some extent. 'As he hath revealed
himselfe unto us, he is conceived as it were, by the backe parts,
not by the Face. Exod. 33.23. Thou shalt see my back-parts, but
my Face cannot be seene, and darkely, not clearly, that is, after
an humane manner, and measure. I. Cor. 13.12. Through a
glasse: darkely, after a sort.'[28]

This partial revelation was to be apprehended through the
Scriptures. That the Puritans relied sternly on the authority of
the Scriptures is indicated by Ames' statement: 'All things
which are necessary to salvation are contained in the Scriptures,
and also all those things which are necessarily required to the
instruction and edification of the Church . . . Hence the Scripture is not a partiall, but a perfect rule of Faith and manners . . .'[29] A reliance on Scriptural authority was not unique
to the Puritans, but their placing of equal emphasis on Old and
New Testament hindered their moving from their understanding of God as Judge and Lawgiver to an understanding of God
as Saviour and Redeemer. Their well-placed sense of awe in the
presence of a majestic partial revelation of God was not tem-
pered by their knowledge of the more perfect Revelation.

2. *Of Man*

The adherence of Covenant theology to the doctrine of original
sin controlled its understanding of man. Man was created good;
his chief excellency lay in the fact that he was created in the
image of God. But man in Adam fell from goodness. 'The Apos-
tacy of Man is his Fall from obedience due to God, or a transgression of the Law prescribed in God . . . Hence was the
grieviousness of this sin, which did not only containe pride,
ingratitude, and unbeliefe; but also by violating of that most
solemne Sacrament, did make shew of, as it were a generall pro-

---

[28] William Ames, *The Marrow of Sacred Divinity* (London, 1639), p. 9.
[29] *Ibid.*, p. 150.

fession of disobedience, and contempt of the whole covenant.'[30] Man's fall can only be attributed to himself and his abuse of his free will.

The consequences of man's fall are guiltiness, filthiness, and punishment. Guiltiness results in an evil conscience, and filthiness is that 'spiritual pollution, whereby a sinner is made destitute of all comliness, and honour, and becomes vile'.[31] The punishment for sin is death, a spiritual death which results in the 'defacing' of the image of God in man, and in his being placed in bondage to the powers of darkness. Man's fall was no mere slip of the foot. 'It is the corruption of the whole man . . . Hence also it is that in Scripture, a *homogeneall* corruption is attributed not only generally to the whole man but also to every part of it: as to the understanding . . . To the conscience . . . To the will . . . To the affections of every kind . . . To uncleannesse in the lusts of their hearts . . . Lastly, to the body and all the members of it . . .'[32] And it is this fallen man who continues to live in deviation from the law of God.

This then was man who was outside the covenant relationship with God – man totally corrupted and totally impotent to aid himself. This same man when he was within the Covenant of Grace was justified and sanctified. 'By justification a believer is properly freed from the guilt of sin, and hath life adjudged to him . . . so by sanctification the same believer is freed from the filthiness and staine of sinne and the purity of Gods Image is restored to him.'[33]

3. *Of Christ*

The unbridgeable gulf separating an eternal, holy and sovereign God from fallen man has been bridged, but only on the initiative of a gracious God who chose to covenant with Abraham and his seed and thereby set man in a new relationship with himself. The mediator and surety of this new covenant is Jesus Christ.

. . . As the Lord Jesus Christ is the first and last in other things,

---

[30] *Ibid.*, p. 49.
[31] *Ibid.*, p. 53.

[32] *Ibid.*, p. 58.
[33] *Ibid.*, p. 125.

so in the Covenant; he doth bring us into God, and to the right of
the Covenant . . . you have no right into the Covenant before you
have him. You have no condition of the new Covenant unless you
have him.[34]

The office of Christ, is that which he undertooke, that he might
obtain salvation for men: I Tim. 1.15. This is a sure saying, and
worthy of all acceptation: That Jesus Christ came into the World
to save Sinners . . . The office it selfe to which Christ was called is
threefold: of a Prophet, of a Priest, of a King.[35]

Despite the seeming orthodoxy of this presentation of the
person and work of Christ, one discovers as one continues to read
Puritan theology that the usage of the concept of covenant to
allow for an acting God and a responding man has relegated
Christ to an inconsequential role. Christ is understood in terms
of the covenant rather than the covenant in terms of Christ.
God has not so much made himself known in Christ as he has
used him to ratify a contract, and therefore both the person and
work of Christ are seen in predominantly static terms. And in-
dispensable as Christ may have been to the Puritan mind as a
pledge of the mercy and faithfulness of God, he was a pledge
of that God whom they had encountered first of all in the Old
Testament.

4. *Of the Church*

The Covenant of Grace which bound God and man to each other
had its social counterpart, a Church covenant. This covenant
was defined by Richard Mather:

A solemne and publick promise before the Lord, whereby a company of Christians, called by the power and mercy of God to fellowship with Christ, and by his providence to live together, and by his
grace to cleave together in the unitie of faith and brotherly love,
and desirous to partake together in all the holy Ordinances of God,
doe in confidence of his gracious acceptance in Christ, bind themselves to the Lord, and one to another, to walke together by the
assistance of his Spirit, in all such wayes of holy worship in him,
and of edification one towards another, as the Gospel of Christ

---

[34] Cotton, *op. cit.*, pp. 222.
[35] Ames, *op. cit.*, pp. 73-74.

requireth of every Christian Church, and the members thereof.[36]

Certainly, on the face of it, this definition of the Church covenant need not have led to a discriminatory membership policy.
However, in moving from definition to actuality, there were un-
fortunate complications. One of these which has already been
mentioned was the inextricably entwined relationship which
existed between the church and state. Lying behind this was the
Puritan understanding of the doctrine of election.

There was no question but that God's calling of man took the
form of election. The covenant doctrine of election was stated:
'Election is the predestination of some certaine men, that the
glorious grace of God may be manifested in them . . . The first
act of election then is to will the glory of his grace in the salvation of some men . . . The second act is to appoint some certain
who shal be made partakers of this salvation . . . The third act
of election is a purpose or intention of preparing and directing
those meanes by which men elected are certainly lead through
to salvation as to an end.'[37] Election, the bestowal of God's grace
on man, called him to a new life and regenerated in him the
power to respond which he had lost in Adam's sin. The regenerate were required to enter into covenant relationship with
others who were regenerate.[38]

The pressing problem lay in the determination of which persons actually constituted the regenerate. It was simple enough
to say that from the side of God's activity the regenerate were
those who were elected to salvation, and it was a foregone conclusion that the original settlers of the Massachusetts Bay Colony
who had covenant together and who were 'this choice grain' sent
'into this wilderness' were of the regenerate. But what about

---

[36] Percy Miller, *The New England Mind, The Seventeenth Century* (Cambridge, Harvard University Press, 1957), p. 735.

[37] Ames, *op. cit.*, pp. 106-107.

[38] *Ibid.*, pp. 142-143. 'So that a more ample and certaine blessing of God may
be expected in the Church of God instituted, than in any solitary life whatsoever. They therefore that have opportunity to joyne themselves to the
Church, and neglect it, doe more greviously sinne, not only against God in
respect of his ordinance but also against their owne soule in respect of the
blessings adjoyned. And if they doe obstinately persist in their carelessnesse,
whatsoever they doe otherwise professe, they can scarce be accounted for
believers truly seeking the Kingdome of GOD.'

their children, the late arrivals, the American Indians who had
the temerity to be there first, and Negroes? In theory this problem was soluble. It seemed logical to the Puritan mind that those
who had experienced regeneration would certainly know of it
and could therefore witness to each other of it. It was on the
basis of this satisfactory witnessing that men would become participants in the Church covenant. The Puritans took into consideration that they were dealing with an incomprehensible God
and that they might err in determining the satisfactoriness of
man's witness, but this prospect did not frighten them so much
as the thought that unless some such precautions were taken,
the 'citty upon a Hill' might contain the unelect.

It is only necessary to touch briefly again on the subject of
the relationship between church and state. This is well-illustrated by one Puritan's description of the Colony: 'I look upon
this as a little model of the Glorious Kingdome of Christ on
earth, Christ Reigns among us in the Commonwealth as well
as in the Church and hath his glorious Interest invoked and
wrapt up in the good of both Societies respectively.'[39] It was
quite clear to the Puritans that the purpose of civil government
was to further the rule and will of God, so the covenant theory
included a civil covenant. Because of the fall of Adam, it was
necessary that there be a coercive power to restrain the evil
impulses of man, and for this purpose God had instituted
civil government. It stood to reason that the elect or regenerate
were better able to perceive the will of God for communal life.
It was in the Scriptures that one discovered this will to which the
laws of society were to correspond, and the regenerate were
equipped to understand the Scriptures. For this reason the franchise was restricted to church members. God created the state
by working through his elect who in turn would preserve for the
non-elect such civil rights as God intended them to have. In
theory, neither the church nor the state was to control each
other; they were to work as partners in furthering the truth.
In reality things worked somewhat differently, but this was a

[39] Quoted with source unidentified in Percy Miller, *The New England Mind,
From Colony to Province* (Cambridge, Harvard University Press, 1953),
p. 131.

sincere effort to establish a form of government which would produce a society redounding to the glory of God.

5. *Of Ethics*

It is necessary now to turn our attention to two concepts within the Puritan ethical system which one would expect to have some direct bearing on attitudes towards slavery and church and/or civil rights for Negroes. One of these is the concept of the neighbour; the other is the concept of the ordering of society.

A *Of the Neighbour*

Covenant theology held that before regeneration all men were equally in a state of sin, and that election was in no way dependent on any quality in man. As Ames stated it, 'for it is sufficient to understand that men are the object of this decree, so that the difference of the decree doth not depend upon man, but that difference, which is found in men, doth follow upon the decree.'[40] That difference is twofold in that the elect are justified (the righteousness of Christ is imputed to them) and sanctified (an alteration of qualities in man himself). In the faithful sin is broken, subdued, and mortified; in the unregenerate sin reigns, prevails, and predominates. Therefore, when covenant theology dealt with the concept of neighbour, it saw the regenerate man as possessing real and tangible qualities which differentiated him from unregenerate man.

Justice and charity were equated as the virtue whereby one was inclined to perform his duty towards his neighbour. The question, 'Who is my neighbour?' was answered by Ames: 'Every man, whom by any meanes we may accommodate, is, in some sort, our neighbour . . . Man in generall, as he is with us capable of supernaturall happinesse, in as much as he is the proper object of Absolute Charity, is our neighbour. For this is the tye of our charity between one another, in order to God whom we love. And thus is every man living our neighbour, without difference of Kind, affection, or manners, unless somewhat to the contrary doe certainly appeare unto us.'[41]

---

[40] Ames, *op. cit.*, p. 105.   [41] *Ibid.*, p. 128.

But 'somewhat to the contrary doe certainely appeare' unto the Puritans almost immediately. Covenant theology found it appropriate to delineate the degrees of love owed to various neighbours. While no man was to be totally removed from the embrace of Puritan charity, 'Among men those are more to be loved than others, that come nearer to God, and in God to our selves,'[42] 'But yet there is some difference of order in the wishing that good: for we ought to wish that happinesse to the godly immediately, but to the ungodly, only hoping and supposing their Faith and Repentance.'[43]

And even among the 'godly' neighbours, there was to be a hierarchy of love. Kindred in blood were to be loved more than strangers, and some special friend was to be loved more than an ordinary kinsman in blood. Parents were to be loved more than friends, and one's parents were to be loved more than one's children in certain respects and one's children more than one's parents in certain respects. Husbands and wives (one's own presumably) were to be loved more than one's parents and children. And finally (and tellingly) a community or society was more to be loved than any member of it.[44] In the construction of this system of degrees of love the Puritan theologian's inability to think in any but the most methodical terms surely reached the point of absurdity. Here he undermined his own and the Biblical understanding of the neighbour as being that person who needs one's love.

Ames devoted a small section in his theological tome to the obligation between masters and servants:

Perfect servitude, so it be voluntary, is on the patients part often lawfull between Christian and Christian, because indeed it is necessary: but on the masters part who is the agent, in procuring and exercising the authority, it is scarce lawful; in respect, it thwarts that generall canon, *What you would have men doe unto you, even so doe unto them*; Matt. 17.12. Perfect servitude, by way of punishment, can have no place by right, unlesse for some hainous offence, which might deserve the severest punishment, to wit, death: because our liberty in the natural account, is the very next thing to life it selfe, yet by many is preferred before it. The condition of those

---

[42] *Ibid.*, p. 301.   [43] *Ibid.*, p. 129.   [44] *Ibid.*, pp. 302-303.

men, who are fore ever bound and enslaved to some certaine kinds of work: And of other servants, who hire themselves out for a time at such or such a price, is not perfect servitude.[45]

There are obviously problems of interpretation here. The inference seems to be that in certain circumstances perfect servitude is justifiable, but there is no precise statement of what constitutes perfect servitude. On the other hand, two conditions which do not constitute perfect servitude are stated with no indication of their lawfulness. The first of these might refer either to slavery or to man's vocation. However, at another point the same writer indicated that the states of servitude and freedom could not be considered in conjunction with a doctrine of vocation.[46] But if the reference here is to slavery, Ames, usually the most methodical of theologians, has not committed himself to any extent. The value of the passage is far more in his demonstration of a Puritan knowledge that liberty was a priceless possession indeed.

B *Of the Ordering of Society*

The Puritans believed that gradations in society were divinely appointed – that there was a fixed ordering which lay within the providence of God and worked to his glory.

Two illustrations will suffice. In a sermon preached on election day in 1676, William Hubbard, one of the most venerated ministers of the Colony, said:

It was Order that gave Beauty to this goodly fabrick of the world . . . The better to understand this we may consider what Order is. Such a disposition of things in themselves equall and unequall, as gives to every one their due and proper place . . . So that it appears whoever is for a parity in any Society, will in the issue reduce things into a heap of confusion. That God who assumes to him self the title of being the God of Glory, is the God of Peace, or Order and not of Confusion . . . It is not then the result of time or chance, that some are mounted on horseback, while others are left to travel on foot . . . Nothing therefore can be imagined more remote either from right reason, or true religion, than to think that because we were all once equal at our birth, and shall be again at our

[45] *Ibid.*, p. 160.   [46] *Ibid.*, pp. 327-328.

C

death, therefore we should be so in the whole course of our lives.[47]

As late as 1740 when Puritanism had undergone significant changes, Jonathan Edwards preached a sermon which seems to have been based on a sociological analysis of Northampton where his congregation was situated. In this sermon he spoke directly to social outcasts which might be taken to indicate their presence in his congregation. He said:

So you that are servants and poor negroes. You are of those who are poor in the world, but harken to the call of Christ, and improve the present opportunity earnestly to seek your salvation . . . Though you are a servant, yet if you will come to Christ, and heartily give up your life to his service, you shall be the Lord's freeman . . . If you refuse to hearken to Christ, and live in the neglect of your salvation, then you will not only be the servant of men, but the servant of the devil, and will hereafter fall into his hands, and be in his possession forever.[48]

The attempt must now be made to find some meaning in these tangled threads. We have seen that the Puritans were not adverse to slave-trading or slave ownership. We have seen that they displayed very little concern for the evangelization of their slaves. We have discovered no attempt on their part to work their way through the theological and political maze which covenant theology produced in terms of the personal and civil rights of slaves. To reiterate this confused situation: Negroes were obliged to enter into personal covenant relationships (as marriage); they were obliged to subscribe to the church covenant in order to become church members but were granted only partial privileges of the church covenant; they were not allowed to enter into the civil covenant (which in the case of whites was automatic upon church membership) but were granted partial citizenship rights. Their obligations were those of all unregenerates so long as they were unregenerate; regeneration

[47] Percy Miller and Thomas H. Johnson, eds., *The Puritans*, Vol. I. Revised Edition (New York, Harper and Row, 1963), pp. 247-249. The fact that Hubbard some years later married his housekeeper perplexed and offended his parishioners.
[48] Percy Miller, 'Jonathan Edwards' Sociology of the Great Awakening', *The New England Quarterly*, Vol. XXI, No. 1, March 1948, p. 72.

endowed them with the obligations of the regenerate but not with the rights of the regenerate.

The study of covenant theology indicates that it was not racist theology as such. Certain of the ethical sections could have been so constructed but they need not necessarily have been. What one must ask, therefore, is at what point covenant theology left itself open to a racist interpretation or could be used as either a justification for a racist society or a palliative for the Puritan conscience. It is when this question is asked that many scholars arrive at the answer that the Puritan doctrine of election which was used to justify a static ordering of society in terms of 'spiritual insight', vocation, and social status must also have been utilized in terms of colour. Certainly one who is familiar with the theology used to justify the present racist society of South Africa might reasonably conclude that an analogy might be drawn between that perverted Calvinism and the Puritan Calvinism. I am satisfied myself, however, that the crediting of the doctrine of election for Puritan racialism is an over-simplification, for what we find when we read covenant theology is not one doctrine gone amiss but a basic and pervasive bent which is not that which one would expect from a concentration upon the doctrine of election.

Covenant theology was not concerned fundamentally with an electing God; its primary concern was with a despairing and impotent man. It was a magnificently detailed and logically constructed system which justified the ways of God to man and only indirectly the ways of man to God. It was not a theology concerned with man's works, but it was a theology concerned with man's salvation.

Covenant theology was anthropocentric – which is to say man was its pivotal point. This anthropocentricism becomes clear when one brings together certain of the themes already elaborated : the doctrine of election became under this covenant theory a private transaction between God and man but with men determining who are the elect; justification which is the work of God was grounded in man's experience and was conditioned in practice by man's ability to testify to it; sanctification became a process whereby man was increasingly constrained towards law obedience; the Church became man's instrument of some men's salvation.

But when one concedes these points, one is placed in an interesting quandary, for anthropocentricism is usually the result of a too high estimation of man. Such is not the case with covenant theology. So it would seem that we are forced back to a reconsideration of the Puritan doctrine of God, and what we discover is that the Puritan's focus on his salvation *was* the consequence of his understanding of God – the God whom he saw only from behind.

Covenant theology concentrated upon man because man could not bear to concentrate upon God. It derived neither its understanding of God nor man from Jesus Christ, in whom alone one meets both God and man. Jesus Christ is not the Mediator or surety of the New Covenant in the narrow sense in which this was interpreted by covenant theology. He is not merely used by a righteous God to seal a contract with an unrighteous man. He is not a stimulus to man's obedient response; he is man's obedient response. In his person God and man meet, and God's covenant with man is consummated.

Because covenant theology did not see that the true man is Jesus Christ, it could view man in primarily sociological and anthropological terms. It was not the doctrine of election which allowed for a static ordering of society and for the mutilated body of Christ which the Church came to be; it was the failure to understand that Jesus Christ is the Elect one in whom all are elected. This knowledge precludes any attempt on the part of man to place or to hold man in 'his place'. The place of man has been taken by Jesus Christ, and in him man's place is now that of a participant in the life and love of God. And this was not a promise for the future but for Jonathan Edwards' 'poor negroes' then and there in Massachusetts in 1740.

II

REVIVALISM AND
THE NEGRO

The world did not stand still to watch the Puritan experiment. Immigrants by the hundreds of thousands flocked to the shores of America, and Colonies spread to the south and west. However, the religious motivation for immigration was not as intense with other colonists as it had been with the Puritans, although some other groups of immigrants brought their own brands of religion with them. As the country expanded in area and swelled in population, the Puritans found it more and more difficult to maintain their unique position as the perfect theocracy after which the world was to pattern itself. Even their next door neighbours in New York, Pennsylvania and New Jersey rejected the pattern. Second and third generation Puritans themselves were partially responsible for the modifications in church and civil life which undermined and finally lay to rest the 'noble experiment'.

The strongest assault on Puritanism from outside was made by the curious phenomenon called revivalism which dominated the religious scene in the United States throughout the 18th and 19th centuries. It is still present today in the person of some revivalists but more importantly in the permanent effect it had on the theology of American Protestantism in its early and most malleable stages. No denomination escaped its influence, and the Negro denominations which were born during its heyday were strongly influenced by it.

The task of tracing the relationships between the theology of revivalism and its ethic in relationship to race relations is diffi-

cult. In the first place, the period in which this movement
thrived encompasses the entire history of the United States
with the exception of early colonization and contemporary
history. The choice of historical events for analysis must be
highly selective and somewhat arbitrary, and even so one must
detach these events from their larger historical context and
examine them in a narrow and specialized way. The risk of sub-
jectivity is great. In the second place, the revivalists with a few
notable exceptions were not inclined to formalize their theology,
so one must search through their sermons and writings to discover what interpretation of doctrines has bound into one bundle
men as disparate as Jonathan Edwards and Billy Graham. To
simplify these problems, we shall direct our attention particularly to revivalism in its earliest stages and to its strongest
19th century manifestations. Such a plan seems feasible in that
the history of racial events in the United States from the Colonial period of slavery through the Civil War, Reconstruction,
and the beginning of legally segregated patterns of life fits rather
neatly into such a division.

The number of slaves in the Colonies steadily increased from
the time of their introduction into Virginia and Massachusetts,
and the first government census, taken in 1790, indicated a Negro
population of 757,000 in a total population of 3,929,000.[1] As has
been previously indicated, the slaves were concentrated in the
southern and western states. The first generation slaves began
their American pilgrimage on the slave blocks of the north and
were carried by enthusiastic plantation owners to the south.
In like manner revivalism was born in the cool north of New
Jersey and Massachusetts and was carried by enthusiastic
preachers and circuit-riders to the warm south and west where
it warmed the cold embers of Calvinist, Anglican and Reformed
religion. Revivalism was born in 1720 in New Jersey and was
christened the Great Awakening. Two ministers are credited
with having assisted at the birth – Theodore Frelinghuysen, a
Dutch Reformed pastor, and Gilbert Tennent, a Presbyterian
minister. Both felt that the lack of religious ardour on the part

[1] U.S. Bureau of Census, *Historical Statistics of the United States, Colonial
Times to 1957* (Washington, D.C., 1960).

of their congregations (and others) was a result of a presumptuous security which allowed them to identify sound doctrine with saving faith. Both felt that this false security should be shattered by preaching which raised the issue of eternal damnation and which forced a decision on the part of the listener. This technique worked so effectively that many new Presbyterian congregations were formed and eventually a new Presbytery which was controlled by the revivalists. By 1791 the enthusiasm of this group had worn thin the frayed nerves of the establishment, and they were charged by the Synod of New Jersey with 'preaching the terrors of the law "in such a manner and dialect as had no precedent in the word of God"' and 'claiming that truly gracious persons are able to judge with certainty both of their own state and that of others.'[2] The revivalists withdrew and formed the Synod of New York which flourished under their preaching.

Meanwhile, things had been stirring in Massachusetts. In 1734 Jonathan Edwards' congregation in Northampton was struck by revival while he was preaching a series of sermons on justification by faith alone — quite the opposite tack chosen by Frelinghuysen and Tennent — and his church was in a state of chronic revivalism from 1734 until 1739.[3] The revival movement was general throughout New England by 1740, and in the following two years between 25,000 and 50,000 persons out of a total population of 300,000 joined churches in New England.[4]

Until 1740 the Great Awakening resembled a series of sporadic bush fires. A revival was apt to break forth at any place or at any time, but there was no raging forest fire. The fire was kindled by the arrival of George Whitefield, the English revivalist who was a co-worker of the Wesleys. Under his preaching the Great Awakening swept the country from Maine to Georgia. Though Whitefield was a Calvinist, his gospel was an intensely individualistic proclamation of the way to escape from eternal damnation. He saw an emotional reaction as the test of conver-

[2] William Sweet, *The Story of Religion in America* (New York, Harper and Bros., 1950), p. 142.
[3] Ernest Sutherland Bates, *American Faith* (New York, W. W. Norton & Co. Inc., 1940), p. 208.
[4] Sweet, *op. cit.*, p. 133.

sion, and his preaching led to some of the excesses for which
revivalism is famous (or infamous).

Revivalism waned after 1760 but came to life again in the
1790's culminating in the Second Awakening in 1800. There
were two distinct phases of this revival, that in New England
which centred in Connecticut, and the frontier revival. The revival in New England was led by Timothy Dwight, the President of Yale College, and it spread from Yale to other colleges
and into the Congregational churches. The Presbyterians were
experiencing 'awakenings' in New Jersey and New York at the
same time, and the Methodists launched an evangelistic crusade
into New England which intensified and contributed to the
general spirit of revivalism. The New England Second Awakening, however, was relatively calm and free from excessive emotionalism.

Not so the frontier revival which was characterized by fren-
zied excitement and emotional outbursts. Although the father
of the Second Awakening in the west was James McGready, a
Presbyterian minister, the Presbyterians and Congregationalists
very soon withdrew from the scene and left it to the Methodists
and Baptists. The revivals took the form of camp meetings
which often lasted as long as a week and which became so popular that in 1811 there were some 400 to 500 held in the United
States.[5] Estimates of attendance at some of these meetings is as
high as 25,000, of whom as many as 2,000 claimed to be converted. Alongside this remarkable record must be placed the
stories of the extraordinary manifestations of physical distur-
bances and sexual irregularities which plagued the camp meetings. However, the Second Awakening with all its problems
and in spite of ultimate abstention by the more stern Calvinist
element spread through Kentucky, Tennessee, Ohio, Western
New York, Pennsylvania, Western New England and the old
south. The evangelical interpretation of the Christian faith
was burning its way into the heart of American Protestantism.

The Second Awakening did not terminate as distinctly as did
the Great Awakening, but the fires were burning low in the

[5] Clifton E. Olmstead, *History of Religion in the United States* (New
Jersey, Prentice Hall, Inc., 1960), p. 261.

1820's until Charles Finney rekindled them with his revival in western New York in 1826. As had been the big-name revivalists before him, Finney was a Presbyterian, and as had been his predecessors, he was under constant attack by the Presbyterian church until he withdrew and adopted Congregationalism. He was the first revivalist who quite clearly saw revivalism as a technique by which sinners could be manipulated towards conversion, and he studied earnestly to discover ways to get a revival going. He was not loath to share the results of his research with his fellow revivalists and later published a series of lectures explaining his 'new methods'.[6] The fire which Finney kindled swept through northern New York, moved eastward through the older sections of the state, and neared the borders of New England. Even those of the Calvinists who were revivalists became uneasy, so a meeting was held with Finney to discuss the 'proper' methods of revivalism. Finney won the day, gave up his settled ministry, and began to hold revival meetings throughout New England, and in New York, Pennsylvania, and Ohio. At the same time sections of Georgia and South Carolina were being 'revived' by other evangelists who had adopted Finney's methods.

Even Finney and his followers could not compete with the economic collapse of 1837, and during the 1840's the attention of people was fixed upon economic and political matters. But the spirit of revivalism triumphed again when the stock market crashed in 1857. This economic catastrophe was accompanied by mass hysteria, one of the results of which was the belief that the crash was the judgment of God on a sinful order. With seeming spontaneity laymen began to gather for weekly prayer in New York City. As the news media carried reports of these gatherings, the movement spread into small towns and rural areas until the entire nation was caught up in revivalism. The outstanding characteristic of this national revival was that it remained almost solely under the control of lay leadership, although as it increased in intensity, the revivalists of the 1830's were invited to preach in various sections.

[6] Charles D. Finney, *Revivals of Religion* (London, Morgan and Scott Ltd., 1910).

The final wave of revivalism in the 19th century followed shortly after the Civil War and was never able to reach the magnitude of previous revivals. It was led by Dwight Moody, a layman, who began his career in England in 1873 and conducted revivals across the United States from 1875 until 1879. Moody followed in the footsteps of Finney in his studied use of techniques and was the forerunner of contemporary revivalism in that he organized campaigns to cover the whole of Protestantism in large cities. The effort to achieve complete spontaneity which was the aim of early revivalists was finally and totally replaced by the utilization of the high-pressure methods of big business. Numbers of Moody-type evangelists roamed the United States during the latter part of the 19th century, and there was an increasing emphasis on showmanship and the theatrical type of preaching which was popular during the Second Awakening.

We must now retrace our footsteps and determine what happened to Jonathan Edwards' 'poor negroes' and their descendants during this era of unprecedented religious enthusiasm in the United States. To do this we must look at both what was being done to Negroes by the society in which they lived and what was being done to and for them by the religious enthusiasts of the churches.

The first census of the United States was not taken until 1790, so population figures prior to that date have been estimated by the U.S. Bureau of Census. However, these figures are accepted by historians as being reliable enough as a basis for the determination of trends.[7] The number of Negroes in the Colonies had increased from 60 in a population of 4,650 in 1630 to 91,000 in a population of 630,000 in 1730. These figures indicate that the slave trade which had begun with the one ship *Desire* in 1638 had indeed become a thriving industry. It is not within the scope of this book to go into a detailed discussion of the conditions in which the slaves lived. The physical life of the slave was very hard indeed as indicated by the very high mortality rate. There is general agreement that those slaves who were house servants

---

[7] We shall use round figures in order to simplify the discussion of population increases. All base figures are taken from the U.S. Bureau of Census report previously cited.

in the north and south fared better that those who were field hands, and that the master-slave relationship often developed into a relationship which exhibited outward signs of a real concern and care for each other on the part of both master and slave. It is also well known that female slaves were used for breeding purposes both for and by their masters, and along with the large increase in slave population, there was a decrease in the amount of pigmentation in the skin of slaves. However, there was no corresponding increase in benevolence as racial lines became less distinct. The child of a female slave was born a slave and remained a slave.

At the time the Great Awakening was born in New Jersey, there were 2,700 Negroes in the population of 30,000. When it moved into Massachusetts, there were in that colony 2,800 Negroes in a population of 114,000. There are no figures to indicate slave conversions, but it is edifying to look at the attitude of the leaders of the Great Awakening. Jonathan Edwards was himself a slaveholder, and there is no evidence that he ever questioned the propriety of slave-holding, though the issue had been raised before his time and had been tentatively discussed by some of his contemporaries. One cannot but note that he was instrumental in carrying into revivalism the 'ever poor negro' mentality of Puritanism which was pervasive long after revivalism had successfully won the day with its doctrine of general atonement. In his treatise written in defence of revivalism, Edwards said:

And, under the Influences of this Work, there have been many of the Remains of those wretched People and Dregs of Mankind, the poor *Indians*, that seemed to be next to a State of Brutality, and with whom, till now, it seemed to be to little more Purpose to use Endeavours for their Instruction and Awakning, than with the Beasts; those minds have now been strangely opened to receive Instruction, and have been deeply affected with the concerns of their previous Souls, and have reformed their Lives, and forsaken their former stupid, barbarous and brutish way of living . . . and many of the poor negroes also have been in like manner wrought upon and changed.[8]

[8] Jonathan Edwards, *The Works of Jonathan Edwards, Some Thoughts Concerning Present Revival of Religion* . . . (London, 1865, 10th Edition, Vol. 1), pp. 33-34.

The attitudes of Edwards' associates, Tennent and Whitefield, are equally revealing. In one of Tennent's sermons he characterized those who were impeding revivalism as 'moral negroes' and 'caterpillars who labour to devour every green thing'.[9] Whitefield was a slave-owner who eulogized slavery for its temporal blessings to masters and its spiritual blessings to slaves. He had established an orphanage in Georgia, and because slavery was not permitted in that colony for the first fifteen years of its existence, he purchased a plantation and slaves in South Carolina to support his orphanage in Georgia. He was a strong lobbyist for slavery, and when in 1750 it became legal in Georgia, he sold his South Carolina property and established a plantation near his orphanage. He believed that slaves were susceptible to conversion and rebuked slave-owners for keeping their slaves in spiritual ignorance. In one sermon he said: 'God is the same today, as he was yesterday, and will continue the same forever. He does not reject the prayer of the poor and destitute, nor disregard the cry of the meanest negroes . . .'[10]

When one turns from the attitudes of these three leaders of the Great Awakening to what was actually happening in the churches, one finds it very difficult to establish any direct relationship between this early revivalism and a concern for the slaves. The evangelization of slaves was still met by the strong opposition of slave-owners. Presbyterian ministers seem to have been the most active evangelists and one missionary in Virginia, Samuel Davies, is credited with having won large numbers of Negroes to communicant membership.[11] The Methodist General Conference did not instruct its preachers to evangelize slaves until 1787, which was some years after the fervour of the Great Awakening had waned. Perhaps the most generous thing one can say about evangelism in this period is that it was no more

[9] T. Scott Miyakowa, *Protestants and Pioneers* (Chicago, The University of Chicago Press, 1964). 'This racism confused with "pure religion" exemplifies the spiritual and ethical obtuseness frequently attributed to revivalistic moralism. Tennent may not have been a racist but his name-calling cruelly insulted the helpless Negro minority in the colonies.' p. 160.

[10] Max Savelle, *Seeds of Liberty, The Genesis of the American Mind* (New York, Alfred A. Knopf, 1948), p. 63.

[11] Olmstead, *op. cit.*, p. 161.

discriminatory against the Negro than had been Puritan evangelism.

During this period the attitude of the Churches towards slavery was one of accommodation to the institution. The first religious body to protest against slavery was the Quakers whose discussions among themselves began as early as 1688 and moved from condemnation of the slave trade to the condemnation of slavery itself. In 1785 they petitioned Congress for the abolition of slavery. The Methodist, Baptist and Presbyterian churches passed resolutions opposing slavery in the latter years of the 18th century, but all were forced later to recede from their positions by their southern membership. It is true, however, that slaves were being freed in the New England states by state legislation from 1774 through 1800. The influence of the churches on the passage of this legislation was probably considerable. But at the turn of the century the institution of slavery for those states which wanted it was secure.

There was, as there generally is, the exception to the rule in the person of Samuel Hopkins, a disciple of Jonathan Edwards. Hopkins was a slave-holder, but when he was called to a church in Newport, Rhode Island, which was the centre of the slave trade, he became a bitter foe of slavery. As early as 1769 he was preaching against the evils of the slave trade, and became noted for his house-to-house campaign in Newport to urge people to free their slaves. He was able to persuade his congregation to go on record in opposition to human bondage. He was the author of several anti-slavery publications and a leader in the movement which resulted in the emancipation of slaves in Rhode Island in 1774. Hopkins has been called the father of the anti-slavery movement in the United States and was undoubtedly the Great Awakening's finest contribution to the cause.

It was not until 1808 that it became illegal to import slaves into the United States. At that time there were approximately 1,200,000 slaves in a total population of 7,225,000. Although the New England states had freed their slaves, the slave merchants did not take kindly to the loss of the large source of income which the slave trade had provided. For a number of years slaves were smuggled into various ports while the authorities looked

the other way. In the eight years following the abolition of the
trade an estimated 15,000 slaves were brought into the States.
After that the number dwindled, and the plantation owners
concentrated on better breeding methods as their outside source
of supply declined.

The fiery spirit of the Second Awakening in the first decades
of the 19th century burned brightly enough to include Negroes
and slaves among the converted. However the 'poor negro' mentality remained steadfast. Charles Thompson, a historian of
the revival movement, in describing a revival in New Jersey
in 1806 said that between two and three hundred were converted
'including drunkards, apostates, infidels, and those who were
lately malignant opposers, and of all conditions, including poor
negroes . . .'[12] In another instance he placed Negroes in a somewhat more respectable category: 'It is a common case for illiterate negroes and little children of five, six, seven and eight years
old, when they get their first comforts, to speak of their views
of the mediatorial glories of Christ . . .'[13]

On the frontier where the camp meetings flourished, special
physical arrangements were made necessary by the presence
of Negroes. There does not seem to have been a stated policy
of segregation until 1864 when the Methodist Episcopal Church,
South, recommended segregated facilities; but Negroes were encouraged to set up their own camps in regions where slavery
was prohibited as well as the regions where it was permitted. As
the enthusiasm of the meeting mounted, the Negro camp section was separated from the white section by a plank partition.
But on the final meeting day the barrier was torn down, and
the 'two peoples joined together in a song festival and "marching
ceremony" '.[14] It seems fairly evident that if the final meeting day
had extended far into the night, the partition would have been
hastily reconstructed. Masters were encouraged to take their
slaves to the camp meetings, and at that point in history were
willing to do so as a result of having been told for a very long

[12] Charles T. Thompson, *Times of Refreshing* (Chicago, L. T. Palmer &
Company, 1877), p. 78.

[13] *Ibid.*, p. 85.

[14] Charles A. Johnson, *The Frontier Camp Meeting* (Dallas, Southern
Methodist University Press, 1955), p. 46.

time that religious instruction would keep their slaves servile and obedient. They probably also suspected that the frenzy of the meetings might serve as a safe and reasonable channel for any dark, hidden passions of the slaves. Often the slaves were preached to and exhorted by members of their own race, at least two of whom, Henry Francis of Georgia and 'Preacher Jack' of Virginia, became so fluent that their freedom was purchased for them.[15]

Though Negroes were still spoken of and treated with great insensitivity, there seems to have been a fairly pronounced concern about their condition on the part of religious groups during the period roughly corresponding with the Second Awakening. There was a noticeable increase in interest in the conversion of slaves, and there was a strong anti-slavery element in both the north and south during the early decades of the 19th century.[16] However, there were at least two developments in the religious community which indicated that the basic attitudes of whites towards Negroes remained relatively unchanged. It was during this period that sanctions for segregation which had previously been based on unwritten code in congregations began to appear in church disciplines, and this encouraged the beginning of an independent church movement by Negroes. The first Negro denomination, the African Methodist Episcopal, was formed in 1816. Also at this time the idea of African colonization first advanced by Samuel Hopkins in the latter part of the 18th century was resurrected. The American Colonization Society was organized in 1817 for the purpose of transporting to Africa free Negroes who by this time numbered over 200,000. But by 1830 the Society had expired due to financial problems and to a shortage of Negroes who wished to be removed. The Society was endorsed when it was founded by the Presbyterian, Baptist, Methodist, Protestant Episcopal and Dutch Reformed denominations. While many people sincerely believed that colonization

---

[15] *Ibid.*, p. 116.

[16] There were state anti-slavery organizations in Kentucky, Tennessee, North Carolina, and Maryland in the second decade of the 19th century. These were supported largely by Quakers and expired by 1834. The first anti-slavery periodical was published in Jonesboro, Tennessee, in 1819. Smith, Handy and Loetscher, *op. cit.*, Vol. II, pp. 167-168.

was the most reasonable answer to the problem that the Negro
posed for American society, it seems probable that many churchmen saw endorsement of colonization as a safe middle choice
between the two evils of slavery and church schism. Still others
saw it as a method of preserving the institution of slavery by
removing the dangerous free Negroes who were generally credited along with white agitators for the inciting of slave upris-
ings. These were in fact not too numerous, but there were
enough plots and rumours of plots in the early 19th century to
keep the white population of the southern states in a constant
state of fear and uneasiness.

This period (1800-1830) has been described as one of gradualism.[17] Voices both within the churches and the civil community
were raised in support of the gradual emancipation of slaves. But
the anti-slavery agitation which had resulted in the emancipation of slaves in northern states had abated. One can see the
pattern by looking at the official actions of the Presbyterian
church prior to and during this period. The first important
action was taken in 1787 when the Synod of New York and
Philadelphia called for the gradual abolition of slavery (which
was still legal in the state of New York but which had been
abolished in Pennsylvania in 1780) and the immediate education
of the Negro to fit him for a responsible position in society. The
General Assemblies of 1793 and 1795 passed resolutions ex-
pressing deep concern over slavery, but these were obviously
carefully worded so as to avoid alienation of the pro-slavery
faction in the churches. No further action was taken until 1815
when a resolution was passed declaring that the slave trade
(declared illegal in 1808) was inconsistent with the spirit of the
Gospel. In 1818 the lines of the General Assembly were becoming clearly drawn. A pitched battle was fought concerning the
disposition of an anti-slavery minister. The pro-slavery forces
won and left the Assembly in triumph. On the last day (which
usually had no important agenda items) the anti-slavery forces
presented a resolution which declared slavery to be a violation of
the 'sacred rights of human nature' and 'utterly inconsistent

with the law of God', and which urged Christians 'to obtain the complete abolition of slavery throughout Christendom'. The resolution was adopted. When all delegates were present, this same Assembly endorsed the American Colonization Society. There was no further action by the Presbyterian church until 1846 by which time it had split on theological grounds into the Old and New School Presbyterians. This theological split also fairly clearly reflected the later schism induced by the Civil War.[18]

Throughout the period of the Second Awakening the southern states were developing an agricultural empire based on the production of sugar, cotton and tobacco, all of which depended on large supplies of slave labour. As the free society of the north and the slave society of the south moved westward, the attempt was made to maintain numerical equality between free and slave states. A crisis arose in 1819 when Alabama and Missouri applied for admission to the union. Both were slave states, and on their admission the slave states would have been in a majority. The northerners opposed the entry of Missouri except as a free state, and for a time the nation was deadlocked. In 1820 the Missouri Compromise was arranged whereby Missouri was admitted as a slave state, and the state of Maine was cut loose from Massachusetts and admitted as a free state. Thus, equality was maintained. At the same time Congress decreed that slavery should be forever excluded from the territory north of the southern boundary of Missouri.[19] So it was that the lines were becoming more clearly drawn in the civil community as well as in the churches. Both the continuing economic and territorial expansion of the United States and the continuing success of the revival movement in the south and southwest led inexorably towards civil and church schism. Those persons in the political arena who worked towards compromise and the proponents of compromise in the churches who urged the gradual abolition of evil were becoming equally ineffective.

The fires of revivalism burned low in the 1820's until they

---

18 Olmstead, *op. cit.*, pp. 365-366.
19 Allan Nevins and Henry Steele Commager, *America* (Oxford, Clarendon Press, 1966), pp. 168-169.

were rekindled by Charles Finney's revival in Western New York in 1826. The blaze which he lit burned across the churches and blazed into an anti-slavery movement of such militance that there was no longer the option of gradualism or moderation. Abolition was no longer a theory to be held but a fact to be accomplished. And as fires will do, this one raged out of the control of those who lit it. Finney is the best known of the revivalists of the 1830's, but the roster of anti-slavery revivalists is a very large one. It included such men as Lyman Beecher, Peter Cartwright, Jacob Knapp, Francis Wayland, Joshua Leavitt (at one time considered by abolitionists to be one of their most able leaders), Albert Barnes, Horace Bushnell, and Henry Ward Beecher. These men were Methodists, Baptists, Presbyterians and Congregationalists. Until the mid-1830's the south produced some anti-slavery revivalists, most notably in the form of Methodist circuit riders. One, James Axley of eastern Tennessee, claimed that 'a preacher that was good and true had a trinity of devils to fight – superfluous dress, whisky, and slavery'.[20]

The story of Finney's relationship to the anti-slavery movement is confusing to the historian who does not understand that his support of abolition was a result of his religious convictions and therefore never *the* primary cause for him that it was for some abolitionists. He stated his position this way:

> When I first went to New York, I had made up my mind on the question of slavery, and was exceedingly anxious to arouse public attention to the subject. I did not, however, turn aside to make it a hobby, or direct the attention of the people from the work of converting souls. Nevertheless, in my prayers and preaching, I so often alluded to slavery, and denounced it, that a considerable excitement came to exist among the people.[21]

His approach led to his being criticized by some of his own disciples as being too moderate in his stand against slavery. However, he was one of the first ministers to exclude slave-

[20] Johnson, *op. cit.*, p. 63.
[21] Charles C. Cole Jr., *The Social Ideas of the Northern Evangelists, 1826-1860* (New York, Columbia University Press, 1959), p. 204.

holders from his congregation, and he was an active vice-president of the Ohio Anti-Slavery Society throughout its existence. One of his chief contributions to the anti-slavery movement was a result of his membership in that organization. At its annual meeting in 1839 Finney presented a series of resolutions which were accepted by the Society and which became the foundation of the 'higher law' doctrine which was subsequently used in most anti-slavery arguments. The resolutions read in part:

Resolved, That for the following obvious reasons, we regard it, as a well settled principle of both common and constitutional law, that no human legislation can annul, or set aside the law or authority of God.

(*a*) The most able writers on elementary law, have laid it down as a first principle, that whatever is contrary to the law of God, is not law.

(*b*) Where a bond, or other written instrument, or anything else, is of immoral tendency, courts of law have refused to recognize it as legal and obligatory.

(*c*) The administration of oaths, or affirmations, in courts of justice, is a recognition of the existence and supreme authority of God.

(*d*) The Constitution of this State expressly recognizes the axiom, that no human enactment can bend the conscience, or set aside our obligations to God.

(*e*) The general instrument on which the federal Government is founded, recognizes the same truth – that rights conferred by our Creator as inalienable, can never be cancelled, or set aside by human enactments.

(*f*) The administration of oaths, or affirmations in all departments of the general and state governments, is a recognition of the truth, that God's authority is supreme.

Resolved, That we deem it highly improper, for Christians to decline acting on the subject of slavery and emancipation, on account of the political character and bearings on these questions, because we cannot innocently suffer legal enactments to crush our brother, when the means of prevention are peaceable, and within our power.[22]

22 *Ibid.*, pp. 209-210.

Less directly but quite importantly, Finney influenced the anti-slavery movement through those who were converted at his revivals. The area in which he preached was the area which seized leadership in the abolition crusade. Among his individual converts who assumed positions of importance in the movement were Theodore Weld who was responsible for turning Lane Seminary into a hotbed of agitation until his and his students' activities were eventually banned; Arthur Tappan, first president of the American Anti-Slavery Society; and Joshua Leavitt, who was editor of two anti-slavery publications. Finney's revivalistic techniques were also adopted by the anti-slavery movement. Revivalist lectures, personal persuasion, and hymn-singing were the popular method of winning converts to the cause of abolition.

Until fairly recently, historians have given credit for leadership of the anti-slavery crusade to the fiery William Lloyd Garrison whose newspaper, *The Liberator*, became the most powerful instrument of anti-slavery propaganda; but it is generally agreed by contemporary historians that Finney and the evangelicals played effective roles. The unity of the movement was destroyed by Garrison who, as a crusader for other unpopular causes such as women's rights, became increasingly radical and intemperate. The crux of the issue between the evangelicals and Garrison's followers was one of method. The most radical of the evangelicals demanded immediate abolition, gradually accomplished, whereas for Garrison 'immediate' meant 'now'.[23] The anti-slavery forces were meeting with increased opposition and some persecution and physical violence, and Garrison's response was to attack all who disagreed with him. He came to see the 'moderation' of the evangelicals and the non-involvement of the established churches as synonomous and equally pernicious. He viciously attacked the church in *The Liberator* and finally ousted the evangelicals from the American Anti-Slavery Society. They reorganized themselves into the American and Foreign Anti-Slavery Society but were never able to regain a position of leadership.

[23] Gilbert Hobbs Barnes, *The Anti-Slavery Impulse 1830-1844* (New York, D. Appleton-Century Co., 1933), p. 78.

Prior to the break one of the issues which had been faced with mixed emotions and confusion was that of social intercourse with Negroes. This was a real dilemma in that such intercourse could lead to violence which could be seen as harming the cause, but the refusal to practise it laid the anti-slavery forces open to the charge of hypocrisy by the pro-slavery forces. The issue was stated by Charles Follin at a meeting of the Massachusetts Anti-Slavery Society in 1836: 'How can we have the effrontery to expect the white slave-holder of the South to live on terms of civil equality with his coloured slave, if we, the white abolitionists of the North, will not admit coloured freemen as members of our Anti-Slavery Societies?'[24] But liberal sentiment did not always prevail. Lewis Tappan suggested that a Negro minister be invited to deliver one of the addresses at the anniversary meeting of the American Anti-Slavery Society, but withdrew his suggestion when it met with considerable opposition. After a heated discussion at an executive committee meeting of the Society at which one member threatened to resign if 'true abolitionism' required social intercourse between Negroes and whites, Tappan said, 'I have observed that when the subject of acting out our profound principles in treating men irrespective of color is discussed heat is always produced. I anticipate that the battle is to be fought here, and if ever there is a split in our ranks it will arise from collision on this point.'[25]

Tappan and Finney became engaged in bitter controversy over the question of mixing Negroes and whites at public functions. Though Tappan had not been successful in obtaining permission for a Negro to speak at the meeting of the Society, he had seen that both a Negro and white choir were seated on the platform. Finney was highly critical of this and intimated that it had helped to provoke anti-Negro riots in New York City. Tappan's argument that the choirs sat on opposite sides of the platform and well separated from each other carried no weight. Weld, who always tried to serve as an

[24] Leon F. Litwack, 'The Abolitionist Dilemma', *The New England Quarterly*, Vol. XXXIV, March 1961, p. 53.
[25] *Ibid.*

intermediary between Finney and Tappan, attempted to do so
again by stating his own views on social intercourse. He
indicated that one should 'take *more pains* to treat with attention, courtesy, and cordiality a colored person than a white
from the *fact* that *he* is colored'. However, the question of
the two races mingling on a social basis was to be decided
on the basis of the long-run effects on the cause. He concluded
that while it would be sinful to be unkind to Negroes, 'there
are times when we *may refrain* from making *public visible
demonstrations* of feelings about differences of color in prac-
tical exhibitions, when such demonstrations would bring down
persecutions on them'.[26]

On the other hand Garrison and the more radical abolitionists
who favoured and practised social intercourse were inordinately
proud of their actions and came to see this as the ultimate mark
of devotion to the cause. It became fashionable in those circles
to stage and attend 'mixed gatherings', and those less courag-
eous abolitionists who did not attend exhibited tremendous
curiosity about the gatherings.

One remarkable exception to the general rule among the
moderates was Gilbert Haven, a Boston abolitionist who became a Methodist bishop after the Civil War. While a student
at Connecticut Wesleyan University, he taught a Sunday-school
class of young women at the Negro church in Middletown, and
wrote his mother (with tongue in cheek, it may be assumed)
that she must be prepared to receive a 'dusky' daughter-in-
law.[27] He began in his first pastorate to denounce slavery, but
his views on race set him apart from most reformers. He believed that caste feeling based on colour was the cornerstone
of American slavery and pointed out that this was in direct
refutation of the Bible which proclaimed the absolute oneness
of man in Adam, Noah, and Christ.[28] In a sermon preached in
1854 he offered the following prescription as the cure for
slavery:

[26] *Ibid.*, p. 56.
[27] Timothy L. Smith, *Revivalism and Social Reform* (Nashville, The Abingdon Press, 1957), p. 220.
[28] Gilbert Haven, *National Sermons* (Boston, Lee and Shephard, 1869), p. 123.

. . . We must do these first duties in politics and in the Church, but we must not leave the great duty undone. We must extirpate this prejudice from our hearts . . . But you may ask, How shall I begin the cure?

1. By resolving to think no more of the color of the skin than you do of the eyes, and to like its color, as you do that of the eyes. Look at the heart, at the divine likeness there, and let your feelings be excited only by sympathy with its virtues.

2. You must be willing to welcome them (Negroes) to your house and table, if they are worthy of such a welcome . . .

3. You must go further than this. They have a right, and ought to be encouraged, to enter the various paths of industry and enterprise . . . You must give them a chance to develop their talents . . .

4. But you will say this social, business and political equality may lead to another, the very thought of which is insufferable . . . So, when you ask us if we believe in the intermarriage of the races, we answer, True marriage is a divine institution. Such hearts are knit together by the hand that originally wove them – in separate but half-finished webs. God makes this unity . . . As it respects such marriage, all I need to say is, 'It is none of our business. It is the business of the two souls that are thus made one by the goodness and greatness of their Creator.'[29]

Haven was obviously a-typical and never became a leader in the anti-slavery movement.

Throughout the 1830's and into the '40's when the witness of the Finney revivalists was most marked, they were never able to win the churches to their cause. One writer has said: 'In the churches the counsels of conservative men prevailed – of saintly leaders whose goals were mystic and otherworldly and of editors and ecclesiastical officials anxious for the peace and prosperity of their flocks.'[30] And another has said: 'Highly placed leaders in all communions except the Friends were, at best, only moderates on the slavery question; that is to say, they generally deplored slavery but hesitated to engage in any decisive or concerted action to liquidate it . . . If . . . major denominations had taken collective action during this period, there is good reason to believe that their sentiments

---

[29] *Ibid.*, pp. 142-146.
[30] Timothy L. Smith, *op. cit.*, p. 183.

would . . . have been overwhelmingly anti-abolitionist.'[31]

However, the anti-slavery agitation of the north led the pro-slavery forces within the churches in the south to marshal and verbalize their justifications for slavery. Their arguments were identical with those Biblical arguments which Samuel Sewall had refuted in the 17th century and were in fact the same arguments offered as justification for the maintenance of segregation in the 20th century.[32] The pro-slavery argument was largely based on Old Testament quotations, whereas the revivalist abolitionists attempted to locate their *raison d'être* in an interpretation of the teaching of Jesus as an ethic of love.[33] When the debate narrowed down to the question of whether or not slavery was sin and unequivocal stands were taken by each side, church schism was inevitable. In spite of the attempts of moderates to avoid discussion of the slavery question at meetings which involved both northern and southern constituencies in the years between 1830 and 1845, both the Methodist and Baptist churches split along sectional lines in 1845. The already-existing schism in the Presbyterian church intensified along sectional lines, but it was not until 1861 that the southern Presbyterian church was actually organized. However, John C. Calhoun, speaking to the United States Senate in 1850 of the impending crisis, pointed out that the only one of the large Protestant denominations which remained unshaken and intact at that time was the Protestant Episcopal. The anti-slavery movement had borne strange fruit within the

---

[31] Smith, Handy and Loetscher, *op. cit.*, p. 174.

[32] For an analysis of these arguments see Everett Tilson, *Segregation and the Bible* (Nashville, The Abingdon Press, 1958).

[33] The writer has had extended conversation on this point with a German theologian, Manfred Linz, who travelled and studied in the United States to obtain material for an article 'Sklaverie als ethischer Modeifall' published in the December 1960 issue of *Evangelische Theologie*. Linz contended that the positions of both the southern and northern groups were ideological rather than theological, the southern position being one of unhistorical Biblicism and the northern one of unhistorical idealism. In his study he found only one noteworthy instance of a 'Christian' stand – a resolution passed by the Synod of Kentucky in 1835 which affirmed their responsibility and guilt and did not, as Linz put it, 'deliver a window-sermon'. The resolution interpreted slavery as robbery, in that no person can own another person unless Christ has given up his right to him.

churches, and the revivalists of the 1830's must be given large credit for the crop.

In the civil community the Missouri Compromise of 1820 had held firm until 1844 when the question of admitting Texas and the states acquired in the Mexican War – California, New Mexico and Utah – arose. Texas already had slavery, so she entered the Union as a slave state. The other states did not, and once again there were years of bitter debate and threats of disunion. In 1850 a compromise was reached which provided that California be admitted as a free state, that New Mexico and Utah be organized as territories without legislation for or against slavery, that the slave trade be abolished in the district of Columbia, and that more efficient machinery be set up for returning fugitive slaves to their owners. For three years the Compromise of 1850 seemed to settle the differences, but the tension beneath the surface continued to mount. Most northerners refused to abide by the new Fugitive Slave Law and actually intensified their efforts to help slaves escape. And the issue of slavery in the territories continued to be agitated by both sides. There was very nearly open warfare between the southern slave-holders and northern anti-slavery men who poured into the new areas of Kansas and Nebraska in an attempt to hold them for their sides. In 1857 the Supreme Court declared in the Dred Scott case that Congress had no power to exclude slavery from the Territories, but the decision was too late and the north too strong. The nation marched on to its rendez-vous with disaster, and on April 12, 1861, the southern guns fired on Fort Sumter.

It is quite clear that the Civil War was not fought on the issue of slavery alone. Most certainly this war, often described as the 'Brothers' War', was not primarily concerned with the ethical implications of the institutions of slavery.[34] Slavery

---

[34] The 'Brothers' War' is not just a romantic misnomer for the conflict between the northern and southern states. Sentiment in the border states of Maryland, Tennessee, Kentucky and Missouri was sharply divided, and if brother did not fight brother, relatives surely fought relatives. In the small Tennessee town in which I lived for many years, two monuments face each other in the court-house square, one a memorial to the Union soldiers and the other a memorial to the Confederate soldiers.

had become an integral part of the economy of the slave states, and these states fought to preserve what was for them the only viable economy. The north was motivated by the belief that that economy was neither viable nor efficient and would in fact, strangle the nation if it were allowed to continue to spread. In the final analysis, the Civil War was a fight to test the strength of the Union. The question which had to be settled by a bloody, family quarrel was the question of what rights states had in their relationship to the central government when there were sharp differences of opinion. The Negro slaves as human beings became very nearly coincidental to the main issue. Even the issuing of the Emancipation Proclamation in 1862 was to some extent a tactical manoeuvre on the part of President Lincoln which was designed to re-inspire the flagging zeal of the Union army when the Confederate Army first invaded the territory of the north and to ensure British sympathy for a 'moral crusade'. The primary question was answered when the southern forces surrendered in April of 1865. The Union was preserved but at such a price that disunion would remain the hall mark of national life throughout ensuing decades and indeed to the present day.

The Civil War and its aftermath which served to intensify and solidify sectional differences in the civil community served the same purpose in the churches. Although the large denominations had split prior to the War and each had offered vigorous support to its 'army' and 'government', it was the 'missionary' activity of the northern bodies in the south which was the ultimate loss of face for the southern churches. This activity which began in vacant southern pulpits during the War was greatly increased during the period of Reconstruction. Feelings hardened to the extent that reunion of the churches became increasingly impossible. To this day only the Methodist church has re-united, and one senses that is more a 'paper' than a real union.

It seems quite reasonable that after an internal war has ripped a country apart steps must be taken to bind it together again. This was one of the primary purposes of the Reconstruction programme which is usually said to have extended from the end of the War through 1877. Another purpose was the obtaining and guaranteeing of the civil rights of the then freed slaves. A great deal has been written about the Reconstruction era and much of it very biased indeed. For our purposes, it is only necessary to point out that neither the victor nor the victim behaved very well during this period. Once again, the Negro became a pawn in the gruesome game of sectional rivalry. On the one hand, his rights as a citizen were bestowed upon him by constitutional amendment – though the written constitution had never deprived him of those rights. The 14th and 15th amendments made clear that the Negro was a citizen whose privileges and immunities could not be abridged by the states. The 15th amendment specifically granted the right of franchise to the Negro. But even as these rights were being formally stated, the strategies for keeping the Negro 'in his place' were being born in the minds of many.

A large share of the northern churches' missionary activity in the south was directed towards the education of freed slaves. The Freedmen's Bureau which was organized by the Federal government and had as one of its primary aims education relied heavily on assistance from the churches. The southern churches also expressed a concern for the education of the Negroes, many of whom were unprepared to care for themselves or their families and many of whom were roaming the country searching for their families which they had lost in former slave sales. The southern churches were true to their historical bent by placing primary focus on religious education, but factors were at work which made that task difficult and unrewarding. Many southern white church members who had lost their fortunes as well as members of their families could no more forgive the Negroes for the war which freed them than they could forgive the Yankees who had won the war, and many whites were determined that the Negroes who were the cause of their disaster should be separated from them. The pattern of segregation within congregations moved towards a pattern of separate congregations. At the same time, many Negroes either chose or willingly accepted this pattern. It does not seem that one can fairly say that Negroes were forcibly ejected against their wishes from southern white congregations.[35] However, the period following the Civil War was one of declining membership of Negroes in white-dominated denominations and one of rapid growth of membership in the independent Negro churches.

Negro historians contend that it is in the crucible of Reconstruction that one finds the beginning of the modern Negro's problem. The abolitionists had won the war, but they lost the peace during the drastic years between 1865 and 1877. After (and to some extent, during) this time the Negro was deserted by a previously benevolent north and was thrown on the strained mercies of a white south which was itself in a ruined condition. The churches were quite unable to assume leadership. As early as 1863 Gilbert Haven summarized their past record and gave them a mandate for the future:

The mission of abolishing slavery was offered to the Church of America, as it was to that of Europe. Theirs was faithful to their trust, ours not. And so God has been compelled to take the work into His own hands . . . I do not say that all the Church was silent

[35] The thesis that such reorganization was the result of easy and unanimous decision or that the motivations for it were simple ones is undone by looking at such statements as the one adopted by the General Assembly of the southern Presbyterian church in 1865:

'Whereas, the coloured people never stood in any other relation to the Church than that of human beings lost with us in the fall of Adam; and redeemed with us by the infinitely meritorious death and sacrifice of Christ, and participate with us in all the benefits and blessings of the Gospel; and whereas, our churches, pastors and people have always recognized this claim to Christian equality and brotherhood and have rejoiced to have them associated in Christian union and communion in the public services and precious sacraments of the sanctuary:

Resolved, 1st, that the abolition of slavery by the civil and military powers has not altered the relations as above defined, in which our Church stands to the coloured people nor in any degree lessened the debt of love and service which we owe to them, nor the interest with which we would still desire to be associated with them in all the privileges of our common Christianity.

Resolved, 2nd, that whereas experience has invariably proved the advantages of the coloured people and the white being united together in the worship of God, we see no reason why it should be otherwise, now that they are freedmen and not slaves. Should our coloured friends think it best to separate from us and organize themselves into distinct congregations under white Pastors and Elders for the present, or under coloured Elders and Pastors as soon as God, in His providence, shall raise up men suitably qualified for those offices, this church will do all in its power to encourage, foster, and assist them.'

and sinful. Many testified, as local bodies, as individual preachers
. . . but no great ecclesiastical body, as such engaged in this work.
They almost unanimously strove against it. They resisted those
who sought to bring them into active and determined hostility to
the sin. They wilfully extracted the vigor from resolutions they
could not table, and carefully abstained from the execution of the
tame decrees they were compelled to declare by pressure of outward
fear, and not of inward inspiration . . .

The Church, as an Anti-Slavery Society, has but little work left
for it to do . . . Yet there is a mission before us as great as that we
have neglected . . . The slave is gone, the negro remains. Many
abolitionists, and all mere unionists and partisans, have fancied
their sole work was to liberate the slaves. It is their least work. We
are to be made one family.[36]

His words went unheeded.

There was all too little time for revivalism during the War
years and Reconstruction. The 1870's produced Dwight Moody,
the forerunner of professional lay evangelists, but his theology
led him to believe that social questions were to be solved by
the conversion of individuals. Moody, who was a lover of
humanity, could not escape (as almost no one could) the 'poor
negro' sermonizing:

Has the Blood touched you? the Blood of Christ makes us one,
brings us into the family of God, and enables us to cry, 'Abba,
Father'. At the time of the American War, during the days of
slavery in America, when there was much political strife and strong
prejudice against the black men, especially by the Irishmen, I
heard a preacher say, that when he came to the Cross for salvation,
he seemed to find a poor negro on one side and an Irishman on
the other side, and the blood came trickling down upon them and
made them one. There may be strife in the world, but those whom
Christ has redeemed He has made one family. We are blood
relatives.[37]

One would wish with a passion near to desperation to find
some justification for such pious pontification, but the fact is
that 'poor negroes' made excellent sermon illustration material
– and that was just about it. The Reconstruction era aroused in
white southern people fear and hostility of such a magnitude

[36] Haven, *op. cit.*, pp. 365-367.
[37] Dwight T. Moody, *The Blood* (London, James E. Hawkins, 1876), p. 21.

that a scapegoat was required and, as in Old Testament time,
it was necessary that he be sacrificed outside the camp. So
the white south began the process of legislating separation
while the white north allowed this and more subtly separated
themselves from Negroes. The church stood quietly by as the
Negroes were re-enslaved in a maze of custom and legislation.
And segregation became the law of the land in 1896 when the
Supreme Court of the United States rendered the *Pussy vs.
Ferguson* decision which set forth the doctrine of *separate but
equal* facilities.

The Theology of Revivalism

It was a long torturous path from Jonathan Edwards' learned,
philosophical, pseudo-Calvinist revivalism to Dwight Moody's
'washed in the Blood of the Lamb' revivalist theology. However, with the benefit of hindsight, one can see that the destina-
tion was very nearly inevitable when the path was selected.
When the chief end of religion ceases to be the glorification
and enjoyment of God, man is always glorified.

It is impossible to explore the intricacies of Edwards' theology here but it seems necessary to say a word for him. He did
not really undermine Calvinism, which had been already dis-
torted by the early Puritans. The theology of John Calvin
was from the beginning of the 'great experiment' used rather
than heard. Edwards devoted his life and scholarly effort to
an attempt to rescue Calvin from his American followers. Unfortunately, he was a victim of his own success, and as the
converts poured into the churches, it became more and more
necessary for him to establish an intellectually acceptable justification for his success. This necessity made strange bedfellows
for him, and in the end his theology became the intellectual
umbrella under which revivalism cowered when it faced storms
in its early days. But it was only in Edwards' time that there
was all that much storm – revivalists were intellectually slack
– and 'non-theology' rapidly became the way of life for American churches. After Edwards' theological tussle with the
methods of the Tennents and Whitefields, the path was clear

for man to 'scramble to the safety' of God's throne.[38] And that Edwards lost the tussle is testified to by later revivalist historians who could say, 'So Whitefield and Edwards, and Nettleton and Baker, and Finney and Hammond and Moody, preach essentially the same doctrines. The differences between them are differences of topics and form, and only in very limited degree, difference of views upon fundamental doctrines.'[39]

The doctrine of salvation was the keystone of revivalist theology. It can be said that a virtue of revivalist preaching was that it was based on a doctrine of general atonement. It is often implied that this was a result of the inability of the revivalists (except Edwards) to work their way through the Biblical doctrine of election, but it is unnecessary at this point to make an issue of this incompetence. The revivalists did, in fact, concern themselves with the salvation of all men. Their emphasis clearly lay on man's personal needs. The satisfaction of man's needs was through a personal conversion experience. Conversion was seen as the turning of the heart to God, and the experience itself was most apt to be abrupt and accompanied by perceptible physical and emotional manifestations of joy and peace. But conversion was generally preceded by a period and state of deep anxiety and fear as the sinner was brought face to face with God. It was the task of the revivalist and the converted to 'pray the sinner through' his anguish to salvation – they became the midwives of salvation.

The revival sermon was the instrumentality by which the sinner was placed in a position where conversion was possible. Calvin Colton, writing in the heat of the Finney revivals, demonstrated the curious mixture of theology and pyschology which underlay most sermons. He explained that both 'the law and the Gospel' are obligatory upon the conscience of man, and that the Gospel is 'clothed with all the sanctions of law'. The showing of the full mercy of the Gospel is 'another and an indirect demonstration of the impenitent sinners exceeding

---

[38] Phrase used by Winslow to describe the revivalist concept of conversion. Ola Elizabeth Winslow, *Jonathan Edwards* (New York, The Macmillan Company, 1940), p. 190.

[39] Charles T. Thompson, *Times of Refreshing* (Chicago, L. T. Palmer and Company, 1877), p. 469.

and infinite guilt is rejecting it'. So far so good. But then things seem to go terribly wrong. 'Every principle of the Gospel writes against him a deeper damnation – dooms him to a lower chamber of the pit of eternal woe. Every bowel of tenderness, which the Gospel opens to him, only proves him more worthy of hell . . . Set up the Cross, and show him a bleeding, dying Saviour, and tell him – tell him with beseeching importunity – tell him with tears – here is blood that cleanseth from all sin! But, by the very supposition of his character, he has refused it – and still refuses. It may be, however, that he will be moved – that he will weep – that he will give up his heart. Try him – try him continually – try him to the last moment of his probation; but do not deceive him.'[40]

Tennent's much earlier revivalism has been described by one writer:

> . . . Tennent chose literally to frighten men into salvation. His pulpit manners were violent instead of persuasive . . . His one theme was hell-fire and damnation. He raged, shouted, stamped, roared, and set nerves on edge beyond endurance. Henceforth, this was to be the revival emphasis.[41]

Tennent's contemporary, Edwards, has been accused also of preaching hell-fire and damnation. However, Edwards saw the wrath of God as intrinsic to his nature and the inevitable result of his rejection of sin, whereas for Tennent there was an absolute dichotomy between the wrath and love of God. The wrath of God became a cudgel which the revivalists used to prostrate men.

Even Dwight Moody, of whom it is said that his central theme was God's yearning love for all men, fell victim to a strange inversion of love and law in his preaching. In what has been called one of his typical sermons, he explained how he had to punish his cross child by refusing to kiss her before she went to school, that they both grieved all day, and that when the child returned asking for forgiveness, he kissed her gladly.[42] So God!! When we are naughty, God withholds demonstrations

[40] Calvin Colton, *History and Character of American Revivals of Religion* (London, Westly and Davis, 1832), p. 256-259.

[41] Winslow, *op. cit.*, pp. 189-190.

[42] Smith, Handy and Loetscher, *op cit.*, Vol. II, pp. 321-324.

of his love from us for a time, during which time we and God are grieved, but when we ask for forgiveness, God gladly responds. One must conclude that for the revivalists law took precedence over the Gospel, and that many interpreted the Gospel itself as a threat rather than a promise.

The question which must be raised when one sees the revivalist emphasis on method and technique is what finally God has to do with the conversion experience. Colton said, 'and although God, in the provisions of the Gospel, – that is, in its entire economy – has come so near to man, as to answer all man's necessities, and as to reserve to himself the glory of the sinner's salvation, he has wisely declined to supersede human agency. In other words – *God has declined to act in the place of man.* He has declined to think, and to feel, and to choose, and to repent, and to believe for him – and all other appropriate parts of man's agency.'[43]

Finney stated his case less blatantly: 'There is a sense in which conversion is the work of God. There is a sense in which it is the effect of truth. There is a sense in which the preacher does it. And it is also the appropriate work of the sinner himself.'[44] Finney explained that the actual turning is the work of the sinner. that the agent responsible for this action is the Holy Spirit assisted by the preacher, and that the sermon is the inducement used by the agent to get the sinner to turn towards conversion. His analogy was of a man who is saved from stepping over the brink of the Niagara Falls by the shout of a person nearby. The man first attributes his rescue to the person, then to the shout of warning, next to his own action, and finally to the mercy of God.

One must say that these typical explanations of the role of God in man's salvation are quite unbiblical. It is evident that this anthropocentric approach would greatly influence other doctrines. Just as the Puritan concept of covenant moulded their theology, the doctrine of salvation played the crucial role in the formulation of revivalist theology.

Man was seen with double vision as it were – as the one to be

[43] Colton, *op. cit.*, p. 208.
[44] Quoted in Cole, *op. cit.*, p. 65.

E

saved and as midwife in the salvation process. As sinner, man was indeed sinful and of lowly estate, but he contained within himself the possibilities of goodness and even perfection. The sinner was freed to these possibilities by the conversion experience which came as the result of his effort and other men's assistance of the Holy Spirit. Such a doctrine of man exalts him to a place somewhere between men and angels.

As man is exalted, the doctrines of God and Christ must suffer the consequence. What seems to have happened in revivalism is that God was split into a God of Love and a God of wrath, and that the God of wrath was obliterated and replaced by a concept — hell, eternal damnation, punishment. The emphasis was not on a God whose holiness was violated by man's rejection of him but rather on the condition of the rejector. This condition was so desperate that man could not deal with it unless he projected a less complicated God, so there emerged the simple, loving God of the revivalists. This God was pliable and controllable, and his love worked more or less automatically. When man repented, the love of God was set in motion. The mystery of the will of God was rationalized, and it became evident that God was the friend of man who helped man achieve the ends he had set himself. The question as to whether or not God's will and man's wishes corresponded was ignored. The God of love could only will love, which was what revivalism aimed to produce.

Developing concurrently with this truncated doctrine of God was a radical 'Jesusology'. One is loath to speak of Christology in connection with revivalism in spite of the revivalists' often-voiced contention that it was Christ and his Cross which should be the most prominent element in revival work. The fact that the revivalists and their sermons served a mediatory function between sinful man and a 'loving' God left no place for the New Testament Christ. In revivalist theology Christ did not do for man what man could not do for himself. He was in no sense true man whom God found acceptable; He was man's 'best friend'.[45] The Cross was no mystery; man had killed his

---

[45] Thompson, *op. cit.*, p. 73. 'He was brought into deep and long despair, but at last God had mercy upon him, and he found in Christ his best friend.'

'best friend' which was, to put it mildly, a dumb thing for him to have done. Repentance, however, allowed him to have his best friend back. That this is no drastic distortion of revivalist theology is confirmed by a study of the preaching and hymnology of revivalism.

When one turns to an examination of the doctrine of the Church, one finds that the church was conceived of in purely functional terms. Thompson makes this fairly clear:

> Human agency then is supported in every revival of religion . . . Thus, however feeble is human agency in itself, God takes it into a glorious partnership . . . We say again, therefore, a church on earth, a company of people allied to God, willing subjects of His grace, willing missionaries of His truth, locking hands with the Spirit, is an essential element in that movement . . .[46]

Finney carried the argument back one step by saying it was the church itself which was the focus of revivals, a church which was sunk down in a backslidden state, and that a revival consisted in the return of the church from her backslidings, *and* in the conversion of sinners. He elaborated:

> When the Church is sunk down in a low state, professors of religion are very apt to complain of the *Church*, and of the low state of religion. That intangible and irresponsible being, the 'Church', is greatly complained of by them, for being asleep. Their complaints of the low state of religion and of the coldness of the Church or of the minister, are poured out dolefully, without any seeming realization that the Church is composed of individuals, and that until each one will take *his own* case in hand, complain of *himself*, and humble himself before God, and repent, and wake up, the Church can never have any efficiency, and there can never be a revival.[47]

> . . . Finally: if they mean to be blessed, let them do their duty – *all* their duty, put their shoulder to the wheel, gird on the Gospel armour, and come up to the work. *Then*, if the Church is *in the field*, the car of salvation will move on, though all hell oppose, and sinners will be converted and saved. But if a Church will leave all the labour to the minister, and sit still and look on while he is working, and themselves doing nothing but complain of him, they will

---

[46] *Ibid.*, pp. 24-26.
[47] Finney, *op. cit.*, p. 253.

not only fail of a revival of religion, but if they continue slothful and censorious, will, by and by, find themselves in hell for their disobedience and unprofitableness in the service of Christ.[48]

Clearly, the Church was seen as a number of individuals attached to each other for the purpose of bringing other individuals into their company. The mystery was removed, and the Church was seen largely in terms of its usefulness to the revival movement. It was in no sense given but was a human device, albeit a necessary one.

It is unnecessary, and would be unrewarding to explore any further the doctrinal basis for revivalist theology. Attempts have been made to understand revivalism as a purely sociological phenomenon, but it was (nor is) not so much that as it was a misunderstanding of basic New Testament doctrines. Prior to the age of revivalism there had at least been a controversy concerning the distribution of power between God and man, but the success of revivalism made the Calvinist case for God more difficult to argue. Also, while the anthropological emphasis of Puritanism did seem to be the end of an attempt to hold in some sort of equilibrium the concepts of the sovereignty of God and the freedom of man, revivalism took the easier path by ignoring the Puritan problem and by assuming man to be in possession of untapped sources of goodness and power.

As has been indicated, the virtue of revivalist theology was that it assumed all men to be equally guilty and in equal need of salvation, and further that salvation was available to all men on the same terms. How then was it able to be of so little influence during the systematic subjection of Negroes throughout the 19th century? There would seem to be three quite basic fallacies in the revivalist theology. Man's salvation was *from* death and damnation rather than *to* life. This inversion of Gospel and law resulted in a moralistic ethic which expended itself in short-term, problem-solving efforts (e.g. the brief involvement of the churches in the abolition movement). This tendency was aggravated by a totally inadequate doctrine of the Church which saw the Church as being a man-made institution rather than as the community, the body of Christ, which

[48] *Ibid.*, p. 279.

transcends all man-made barriers. If men are not *made* the Church, they *make* the Church, and to their own design and specifications. And finally, this man-centred religion could not achieve even the ethical strength of a true humanism because it was based not on a belief in the intrinsic dignity of man but on his capacity for self-improvement. Men might stand on equal footing in their sin but their salvation was a different matter. Since each man was his own representative before God (and not Christ the representative of all) the way was still open for human (or inhuman) categorizing, and revivalism was unable to move beyond the 'poor negro' mentality of the previous decades.

III

THE SOCIAL GOSPEL AND
THE NEGRO

Yes, and there has never been a day since Jesus was lifted upon Calvary when this life of Jesus, simple, human, brotherly, held so commanding a place in the thoughts and affections of the human race as it holds today, never a day when he was speaking through so many lips his messages of good will and peace; never a day when it was so plain that the way of Jesus is the way of life for the world.

From lectures of Washington Gladden in 1913.[1]

There are no Government positions for Negroes in the South, *declared the Collector of Internal Revenue for Georgia in 1913.* A Negro's place is in the cornfield.[2]

Fifty-one Negroes were lynched in the United States in 1913.[3]

The most remarkable period of unconcern about race relations in the history of American Protestantism is that period when the Social Gospel movement was at its zenith. It is remarkable because the Social Gospel movement was by definition (its own) an attempt to apply the 'simple' teachings of Jesus to the life of man in all its ramifications and complexities. As we shall see, its advocates constantly (and rightfully) stressed the wholeness of life, but as we shall also see, they virtually ignored the divisiveness of the racist doctrines which flourished in their midst.

[1] Washington Gladden, *A Modern Man's Theology* (London, James Clarke & Co., 1914), p. 145.

[2] Quoted in Thomas F. Gossett, *Race, The History of an Idea in America* (Dallas, Southern Methodist University Press, 1963), p. 279.

[3] Jerome David, *The Negro in American Life* (New York, The Century Company, 1926), p. 123.

There is very little agreement among church historians on the questions of definition or dates for the Social Gospel movement. As to definition, one can argue that the Social Gospel never really got off the ground if one accepts the very narrow definition of it as an attempt at Christian Socialism (which some of its leaders saw it to be). On the other hand, something did happen – some things were preached or said – which decisively influenced Protestantism in the United States. It seems more realistic, therefore, to accept a rather broad definition of the movement and more fair to accept one formulated by a member of the movement rather than its interpreters. So let us take as a working definition that of Shailer Mathews: 'The application of the teaching of Jesus and the total message of the Christian salvation to society, the economic life and social institutions such as the state, the family, as well as to individuals.'[4] It should be said, however, that the leaders of the Social Gospel movement were not particularly interested in the question of definition. They were convinced that the Social Gospel was *the* Gospel, and they saw themselves not as part of a movement nor as purveyors of any new theories, but as ones who understood the message and implications of the New Testament and wished their understanding to become determinative for the lives of the churches.

There are two theories concerning the date of birth of the Social Gospel movement and its demise. At one time the movement was considered to have been confined to the rather narrow period of the last decade of the 19th century and the first three decades of the 20th. Later scholarship finds the Social Gospel in embryonic stage in the churches as early as 1865 and sees contemporary theology in the United States as being dominated by a modified Social Gospel emphasis. Supporters of the former theory contend that the movement was specifically a response to industrialization which, while increasing after the Civil War, did not reach a stage where there was a reaction to the wholesale social upheaval which it produced until the turn of the century. They further contend that the Protestant

---

[4] Quoted in Willem A. Visser 't Hooft, *The Background of the Social Gospel in America* (Missouri, The Bethany Press), p. 16.

ministry became increasingly conservative after the Civil War.
Hofstadter says that during the industrial conflicts of the 1870's
and 1880's the Protestant ministry was a 'massive, almost un-
broken front in its defence of the status quo'.[5] He sees no substantial reversal of opinion on the part of ministers until the
late 1890's.[6] But Timothy Smith's exhaustive study of the
relationship between revivalism and social reform has generally
won the day for his point that the Social Gospel movement was
born much earlier.[7] Although the revivalist concept of social
action was largely one of benevolence and although the revivalists believed the individual's conversion to be the locus for
social change, revivalism found itself in the case of the anti-
slavery movement pushed towards efforts at a wholesale modifi-
cation of society. Both Finney and Moody emphasized the
necessity for some type of applied Christianity which was not
entirely individualistic. So one would have to go so far with
Smith as to say that the ethical impulses which emanated from
revivalism at least prepared the way for the more stringent
Social Gospel movement. And while at one time it was said
that the movement died during the irreligious 1920's, it is now
generally accepted that it was merely dormant during that
decade of rampant secularism and came to life again in the
1930's and continues to live today.

Let us look briefly at the general situation in American
society which is credited with having produced the Social
Gospel movement before we turn our attention to the specific
question of the Negro's status in that society. Industrialization,
the growth of corporations and a concomitant concentration of
wealth, urbanization, increased mobility, immigration, depersonalization, the formation of labour unions – all of these

[5] Richard Hofstadter, *The Age of Reform* (New York, Alfred A. Knopf,
1955), p. 149.
[6] *op. cit.*, p. 150. Hofstadter's most interesting thesis is that the clergy did
not turn to reform and social criticism solely as a result of 'their disinterested
perception of social problems and their earnest desire to improve the world',
but that they had lost their positions as moral and intellectual leaders due to
the increasing secularization of American life and had also suffered economic-
ally as had all middle-class elements. Their involvement sprang from the fact
that they were themselves members of the disinherited group. p. 151.
[7] Timothy L. Smith, *Revivalism and Social Reform* (Nashville, The Abingdon Press, 1957).

contributed to the fashioning of a society in which the voices of the churches had become increasingly muted. The churches were largely middle-class institutions, and the new working class seemed in danger of seeking its salvation in labour unions. The leaders of the labour movement were understandably hostile to the churches which tended to represent the vested interests of capitalism. As labour and management pitted themselves against each other in the early stages of unionism, strikes and waves of violence swept the country. The early Social Gospel movement was the response of a few prophets within the churches to the new economic and social problems which faced the churches and American society.

The leaders of the Social Gospel movement were not reticent in their diagnosis of the ills of American society. An intensive analysis of their primary concerns has been made by Charles Hopkins. In its earliest phase the movement saw three major problems: unrestricted competition, the conflict between labour and capital, and the problems of urban life with primary focus on the absence of relationship between the churches and the masses. In the 1880's clergymen also concerned themselves with the problems of monopolies, politics, family life, immigration and crime. In the 1890's the list was extended to include war, divorce, civil service reform and populism. These problems continued to occupy the attention of the socially-minded clergymen into the 20th century. One would like to be able to say that there was no specific concern with the problems of Negroes because theirs were the problems of society in general, but this was obviously not true. In 1906 a Congregational pastor at the University of Wisconsin conducted a Social Problems Group in which the Negro was considered one of the problems. And the Sagamore Sociological Conferences which were conducted between 1907 and 1917 added to the usual Social Gospel concerns sex, liquor, advertising and race psychology.[8]

What were the unique problems which the Negro faced during the period when the Social Gospel movement was the dominant force in Protestantism? As was indicated in the pre-

[8] Charles H. Hopkins, *The Rise of the Social Gospel in American Protestantism, 1865-1915* (New Haven, Yale University Press, 1940), *passim*.

vious chapter, the years following Reconstruction were years
during which the Negro was slowly re-enslaved by social,
economic, political and legal measures.[9] This re-enslavement
reached its culmination in the last decade of the 19th century
with the Supreme Court decision in the case of *Plessy vs.
Ferguson* legalizing 'separate but equal' facilities in transportation. Arnold Rose says of this period: 'The position of the
Negro . . . reached its low point around 1900. It was then that
segregation was most complete, violence outside the courts
and mistreatment within the courts the most extreme, the vote
for the Negroes almost non-existent, occupational restrictions
most stringent, public facilities least available, the minority
group most leaderless and voiceless.'[10]

The leadership of the Negro people at that time rested
almost solely with Booker T. Washington, the founder of the
Tuskegee Institute in Alabama. There has been much argument
concerning the merits of his leadership, and it is highly possible
that he was misunderstood both by the white southerner who
accepted him as a 'good' Negro leader and by the Negro who
considers him to have been an 'Uncle Tom'. But Washington
did appear willing to operate within the framework of segregation and to place his hope for the advancement of the Negro
in industrial education. He believed that such education would
eventually obtain for the Negro a measure of economic security,
and whether or not he envisioned this as eventually resulting in
the Negro's bursting the bonds of segregation is a moot
question. At any rate, Washington's famous speech in Atlanta
in 1895 in which he said to an audience of whites and Negroes,
'In all things social we can be as separate as the fingers, yet one
as the hand in all things essential to mutual progress', followed

[9] C. Vann Woodward in his *The Strange Career of Jim Crow* (New York,
Oxford University Press Galaxy Book, 1957), has proved conclusively that this
process was a slow one, that the quarter-century following the Civil War had
seen a considerable relaxation of the barriers between the races in the south
and that it was only when the liberal forces in the north dropped their interest
in the Negro that southern racism and fanaticism took over. It was then that
the hooded Ku Klux Klan first moved openly across the south spreading its
waves of terror.

[10] Arnold Rose, *The Negro in America* (Boston, The Beacon Press, 1956),
p. xxi.

the next year by the *Plessy vs. Ferguson* decision, was instrumental in arousing the first modern voice of Negro protest, the *Guardian*, a Negro newspaper founded in Boston in 1901. The newly militant voice of the Negro found its leadership in W. E. B. duBois, a sociologist at Atlanta University, whose outspoken rejection of segregation so endangered the finances of the university that he resigned his position. DuBois met with a group of Negro intellectuals in 1905 with the hope of forming a national protest organization to wage an all-out battle against segregation and the conciliatory policies of Washington. The group held three meetings but was unable to mobilize any mass following. However, this movement brought into open conflict the two types of Negro strategy, the one stressing accommodation and the other protest, which prevailed throughout the first half of the 20th century. It also provided the nucleus of Negroes who joined with white northerners in organizing the National Association for the Advancement of Colored People following the Springfield race riot in 1908. In 1911 the National Urban League was organized by Negroes and a number of white philanthropists, social workers, and professionals who were interested in the improvement of economic conditions among urban Negroes. The first decade of the 20th century was characterized by the emergence of a fighting spirit among Negroes not unlike that of the slave revolts except that the leadership came from the Negro intellectuals rather than the Negro clergymen. However, the co-operating (and sometimes initiating) element in the white community was not from the ranks of the Social Gospel leadership. And one is hesitant to emphasize white co-operation in the face of the fact that eleven hundred Negroes were lynched in the years between 1900 and 1914.[11]

During the years between 1910 and 1940 three clearly discernible factors were at work which would bring about a change in racial patterns and structures. These were war, migration, and economic depression.

Despite the fact that living conditions were more favour-

[11] C. Eric Lincoln, 'The Black Muslims', *The Progressive*, December 1962, p. 43.

able for Negroes in the northern states than in the south,
Negroes remained concentrated in the south until 1915. Over
90% of the Negro population lived in the southern states in
the year 1910. In the early part of the 20th century there was
relative job security for the Negro in the south. Although there
was a decline in agricultural opportunity, all of the menial
jobs were considered 'Negro' jobs, and the poorest white labour
would not occupy them. And as the Industrial Revolution
reached into the south, the white labouring class began to
receive training to qualify it to fill the unskilled and semi-skilled
positions in industry. Negroes were not trusted with machines,
and most of the Negroes who attended trade schools, which
was where the emphasis was placed in Negro education, ended
up teaching school or doing some sort of menial work.

But then came World War I. The year 1915 is known as the
year of the Great Migration. Estimates of the number of
Negroes who migrated to the northern urban areas in 1915
range from one million to two-and-quarter million.[12] The Negro
was unsettled like all Americans by the war and by the changing
industrial system in the south, and for the first time there was
competition between north and south for Negro labour. Labour
agents poured into the south from the north with promises
of high wages and good jobs, and the Negro press painted
a compelling picture of northern prosperity. Whole clans packed
their meagre possessions and moved north, motivated by the
desire for both economic and social improvement. The southern
farmers attempted to stem the tide by their traditional methods
of coercion and violence, but they were met with grim and
renewed determination on the part of the Negro to escape. The
migration continued in waves, so that by 1940 24% of the
Negro population of the United States was located out of the
southern states.[13]

Another force was at work to increase the Negroes' dissatisfaction with the prevailing patterns of segregation and
discrimination. Almost 400,000 Negroes were drafted in World
War I, and 200,000 went overseas. Only a few saw active duty,
as most of them were used in segregated labour battalions.

[12] *Ibid.*   [13] Rose, *op. cit.*, p. 63.

But there were a few Negro officers, and white soldiers were seen saluting them. And the Negroes who went to France saw for the first time a white people who were only mildly touched with prejudice against them. Negro soldiers returned to the United States in a militant mood and determined to win for themselves the first-class citizenship which they felt was due to those who had fought 'to make the world safe for democracy'. That the militancy of the returning Negro soldier would have been met with oppressive measures in any circumstances cannot be doubted, but it emerged during the post-war depression. The Negroes who had been welcomed in the north during the war found their new footholds in industry being contested by anxious white job seekers, and thousands of Negro workers were fired and replaced with white workers. A wave of lynchings swept the south, and even more bloody race riots swept the north. The summer of 1919 became known as the 'Red Summer'. The membership of the Ku Klux Klan reached its peak at that time and is reported to have been around 5,000,000.

There were three movements of some importance in response to the period of widespread violence and terror. One of these was the Garvey movement. Marcus Garvey, a West Indian, organized the Universal Negro Improvement Association. He renounced all hope of assistance and understanding from the white American, and he also denounced the Negro leadership. His appeal was to the common Negroes whom he urged to flee from the United States and return to Africa. He published a newspaper as the official organ of the movement and organized a number of co-operative business enterprises. His movement which reached its peak in 1920 and 1921 was strong in many parts of the country. The Garvey movement collapsed when Garvey became entangled in financial and legal complications and was deported from the United States on the charge of using the mails to defraud. The major import of the Garvey movement, however, was to demonstrate that there was deep dissatisfaction among the Negro masses and that it was possible to reach these masses.[14]

The second of the movements which was born in response

14 Rose, *op. cit.*, p. 243.

to the violence and despair was what is now known as the Black Muslim movement. It was at that time in the oppressive ghetto life of Detroit that there appeared a man who preached that the battle of Armageddon was to be the black man's final confrontation with the white race which had so long oppressed him. He was at first thought to be a Prophet, but after he disappeared, his followers claimed he was Allah. As Lincoln has said, 'It is an interesting historical phenomenon that when a people reach the precipice of despair, there is so often waiting in the bushes a saviour – a messiah who promises to snatch them back from the edge of the abyss and turn their grief into greatness.'[15]

In 1919 the first southern inter-racial committee, the Commission on Interracial Co-operation, was organized in Atlanta, Georgia. Its purpose was to attempt to cope with the racial antagonism which had been rapidly growing since the war. But by far the most astounding activity connected with it was that of another group led by one of the founders of the Commission. Mrs Dorothy Tilly, with the help of a few other Protestant women, organized the Association for the Prevention of Lynching. The primary reason given by southern white men for lynching Negroes was that that form of disciplinary action was necessary for the protection of fragile and cherished 'Southern Womanhood'. Mrs Tilly and her little band of cohorts, who were in appearances the epitome of that womanhood, made speeches, wrote pamphlets, and literally invaded any area where they suspected a lynching was going to occur. Many a county sheriff was led to doubt the fragility of these women who opposed the Ku Klux Klan when the most liberal of the southern newspapers were silent in the face of lynchings, and the decrease in lynchings can be attributed to a large extent to the efforts of those women. There was one final upsurge of lynchings in the early years of the 1930's, but it diminished quickly both as a result of the continued activity of organizations opposed to lynching and because the south was virtually immobilized by the depression.

This very brief sketch is only indicative of the condition of

[15] Lincoln, *op. cit.*, p. 43.

Negroes in the period when the Social Gospel movement reached its height of influence, but it would suggest that the problems engendered by segregation might have been a viable concern of the Protestant churches.

What was the response of the Social Gospel movement to the plight of the Negro? We shall turn, as we have previously, to the expressions of concern by its leaders. First, let us remember that the early Social Gospel leaders had set for themselves the task of coming to grips with new scientific, social and economic ideas, and such was not within the traditional province of the clergy. Therefore, they are to be commended for their courage even as one must admit that they failed in their intellectual activity. For the purposes of our concern, their most drastic error lay in the area of science. They uncritically accepted an interpretation of the doctrine of evolution which seemed to have as one of its necessary concomitants the idea that human races represented different stages of evolution and were therefore innately unequal. To have denied the superiority of the Anglo-Saxon would have been to have flown in the face of scientific fact and to have identified oneself with the Biblical literalists who were the bane of the Social Gospel movement. Not to question this alleged superiority placed them in the camp of the racists.

The gentle Horace Bushnell writing in 1861 had this to say of 'inferior' races:

A savage race is a race bred into low living, and a faithless, bloody character: The instinct of law, society, and order is substituted, finally by the overgrown instincts of prey, and the race is lost to any real capacity of social regeneration; unless they can somehow be kept in ward, and a process of training, long enough to breed in what has been lost. A race of slaves becomes a physiologically servile race in the same way.[16]

And this to say of the Christian community:

. . . (it) stands among the other bodies and religions, just as any advanced race, the Saxon for example, stands among the feebler, wilder races, like the Aborigines of our continent; having so much

[16] Horace Bushnell, *Christian Nurture* (New Haven, Yale University Press, 1947), p. 172.

power of every kind that it puts them in shadow, weakens them, lives them down, rolling its over-populating tides across them, and sweeping them away, as by a kind of doom. Just so there is, in the Christian church, a grand law of increase by which it is rolling out and spreading over the world. Whether the feebler and more abject races are going to be regenerated and raised up, is already very much of a question. What if it should be God's plan to people the world with better and finer material?[17]

It has been said of another Social Gospel leader, Josiah Strong, that he was 'the clergyman who did the most to correlate his optimistic conviction that the Anglo-Saxon was a superior race designed by God to conquer and populate the world with theories of evolution and social Darwinism'.[18] Since Strong was an official of the Congregational Home Missionary Society, he was in a unique position to publicize his point of view through speeches and writing. His most influential book was *Our Country* from which the following exerpts are taken:

. . . That means that most of the spiritual Christianity in the world is found among Anglo-Saxons and their converts; for this is the great missionary race . . . Evidently it is chiefly to the English and American peoples that we must look for the evangelization of the world.

. . . And it is possible that, by the close of the next century, the Anglo-Saxons will outnumber all the other civilized races of the world. Does it not look as if God were not only preparing in our Anglo-Saxon civilization the die with which to stamp the peoples of the earth, but as if he were also massing behind that die the mighty power with which to press it?

. . . It seems to me that God, with infinite wisdom and skill, is training the Anglo-Saxon race for an hour sure to come in the world's future . . . Then this race of unequalled energy, with all the majesty of numbers and the might of wealth behind it – the representative, let us hope, of the largest liberty, the purest Christianity, the highest civilization – having developed peculiarly aggressive traits calculated to impress its institutions upon mankind, will spread itself over the earth.

. . . It seems as if these inferior tribes were only precursors of a superior race, voices in the wilderness crying: 'Prepare ye the way of the Lord!' . . . Whether the extinction of inferior races before

17 *Ibid.*, p. 180.
18 Thomas F. Gossett, *op. cit.*, p. 185.

the advancing Anglo-Saxon seems to the reader sad or otherwise, it certainly appears probable.

. . . And our plea is not America for America's sake; but America for the world's sake. For, if this generation is faithful to its trust, America is to become God's right arm in his battle with the world's ignorance and oppression and sin.[19]

While most clergymen did not follow Strong in his zealous and blatant racism, neither did they criticize him. From such Social Gospel leaders as Washington Gladden and Walter Rauschenbusch there was no rebuke – perhaps because they had become accustomed to throwing in their lot with men within the church who were poles apart from them in their theological and economic liberalism.

Gladden's own attitude was one of relative confusion. He never directly asserted his belief in the innate inferiority of Negroes, but he quoted with apparent approval men who did say or imply that Negroes were innately inferior. In his discussion of the Reconstruction Era in his *Recollections* published in 1909 he said:

The people of the North were responsible for having given the negro his freedom, and they were bound to see that it did not prove a curse to him. Nevertheless, it was a sad muddle they made of it. To imagine that it was possible, by any political device whatever, to invert the natural order of society, and give to the ignorance of the community the supremacy over its intelligence, was an infatuation to which rational legislators ought not to have been subject . . . The reconstruction measures . . . were based on the disenfranchisement of the people of intelligence and character, and the enthronement of the illiterate and degraded . . .[20]

But in a later chapter dealing with the question of the education of Negroes in the south, he said:

If the main thing to be done for the negro is to keep him in ignorance and subjection, that is a task which requires no great amount of art – nothing but hard hearts and brutal wills . . . We

[19] Josiah Strong, *Our Country* (reprint of 1891 edition by Cambridge, Harvard University Press, 1963), pp. 201, 205, 213-214, 215, 253.

[20] Washington Gladden, *Recollections* (London, Constable and Company Ltd., 1909), p. 179.

F

have had our admonition already . . . If we are not satisfied with
that, if we insist on trying the same experiment over again in a
slightly different form, another day of judgment will come and will
not tarry . . . The stronger race that tries to treat the weaker not as
an end, but as a means to its own selfish ends, plucks swift judgment
from the skies upon its own head . . . There are men at the South
today who know and say that the task which the negro presents to
the South and the nation is not the task of keeping him in subjection, but the task of lifting him to manhood and giving him the
rights and responsibilities that belong to a man.[21]

Rauschenbusch's statements on race were marred by uncer-
tainty and feebleness and sometimes revealed a racial bias. An
example which he used in a book in 1907 is indicative:

How would we feel if a preacher should use a public gathering on
Decoration Day or Thanksgiving Day to predict that *our country*
for its mammonism and oppression was cast off by God and was to
be parcelled out to the Mexicans, the Chinese, and the Negroes?[22]

This bias was probably subconscious, however, as Rauschenbusch generally expressed goodwill towards all races and in
a few instances openly expressed concern about the racial
situation. In the same book he said:

We can now see that a little more wisdom and justice on both
sides might have found a peaceable solution for the great social
problem of slavery. Instead of that the country was plunged into
the Civil War with its fearful cost in blood and wealth. We have
been cursed for a generation with the legacy of sectional hatred,
and the question of the status of the black race has not been solved
even at such cost. If Pharaoh again hardens his heart, he will again
have to weep for his first-born and be whelmed in the Red Sea. It
is a question if we can rally enough moral insight and goodwill to
create a peaceable solution, or if the Bourbon spirit is to plunge our
nation into a long-continued state of dissolution and anarchy which
the mind shrinks from contemplating. The influence of the Christian
ministry, if exercised in the spirit of Christian democracy, might be
one of the most powerful solvents and the decisive influence for
peace.[23]

21 *Ibid.*, pp. 371-372.
22 Walter Rauschenbusch, *Christianity and the Social Crisis* (New York, The
Macmillan Company, 1907), pp. 37-38. My italics.
23 *Ibid.*, p. 369.

One cannot fail to note that the tenor of the statement is such as to exhibit more concern for the welfare of the nation than for the welfare of the Negro race. In a booklet published seven years later, Rauschenbusch indicated the basis for a Christian concern with race relations but offered no guidance to ministers who might have been concerned about widespread rioting and lynching:

> Christianity stands for the doctrine that we must love one another – all men, without distinction of 'religion, race, color or previous condition of servitude'. It will tolerate no exempt breed of supermen . . .[24]

The inability of the early Social Gospel leadership to work its way through the implied conflict between a new scientific doctrine and the Biblical understanding of man makes it at least intellectually understandable that the tragic existence of the American Negro did not become its primary concern. American theologians were not alone in their inability to see beyond the spirit of the day which was one of inordinate racism. They also were in the position of being faced with a society rent by other tremendous problems and could therefore justify to themselves their negligence of one. It was in facing the other iniquities of society that they made an indirect contribution to the churches' involvement with racial problems. It was largely because of their agitation and needling that the churches began to accept (with considerable reluctance) the fact that they owed a responsibility to society which could not be exercised entirely in terms of individual action. In the early years this was conceived to mean that the churches must address themselves to society in some sort of *quasi*-official voice, and they chose to do so through the process of pronouncement-making by official representatives of the denominations. There are many who would question the wisdom of the churches having embarked on that path. There were, of course (and still are), those who believed that the churches' influence in society was best made felt by the interpenetration of society

---

[24] Quoted in Benson Y. Landis, *A Rauschenbusch Reader* (New York, Harper and Bros., 1957), p. 87.

by Christians. On the other hand, many who believed that the
church should be actively involved in society believed that the
pronouncement-making process was a mere cover-up for its
inactivity. However, even if one must share the latter point of
view to some extent, one can hardly doubt that the words of
the churches have in some instances borne weight and contributed towards social change.

The denominations were extremely slow to move into the
area of race relations in their pronouncement-making. There
were approximately 1,100 lynchings in the United States between the years 1900 and 1914, and there were six major race
riots between 1908 and 1920. The first word from the churches
was spoken in 1919 at the climax of the Red Summer. The
Federal Council of Churches of Christ in America, which was
at that time composed of 25 denominations, issued a statement
which urged the abolition of lynching and called for the
recognition of Negroes as Americans and fellow citizens. In
the next ten years most of the large denominations passed
resolutions opposing violence and racial discrimination. However, these were all very general, and none raised the issue of
segregation or responded to the raising of it by various leaders
of the Negro community. In 1927 the Federal Council of
Churches issued a statement in which it attacked the assump-
tion of inherent racial superiority, but it did not draw from
this what would seem to have been the obvious conclusion –
that racial segregation was unnecessary and unjustifiable. One
writer's comment on the churches' few pronouncements during
the first thirty years of the 20th century was, 'Since religious
groups adopted during this time resolutions on a variety of
problems . . . there is considerable justification for observing
that by the silence of most of its bodies Protestantism gave
the appearance of having consented to what was happening
to Negroes.'[25]

During the 1930's there was an increase in the number of
church pronouncements concerned with race relations. Of the
more than 600 social pronouncements adopted by the major

[25] Frank S. Loescher, *The Protestant Church and the Negro* (New York,
The Association Press, 1948), p. 30.

denominations, 40 declarations with 60 endorsements had the racial issue as their subject.[26] The pronouncements were couched in quite general terms as they had been in the 1920's. A majority of the statements focused on the evils of lynching which was already declining. The major problem faced by the Negro in the 1930's, other than the denial of his humanity by segregation, was the economic one because the depression laid an exceptionally heavy burden on the Negro worker who was at the bottom of the salary scale and who was always the first discharged in periods of economic crisis. Only two denominations noted this problem in their pronouncements. During this period the Federal Council of Churches did not pursue its earlier questioning of racial superiority or inferiority, though its realistic pronouncements in other fields were gaining for it a reputation of being a radical organization. The first breakthrough came in the form of pronouncements by the Congregational Church and the Northern Baptist Convention in 1934 and 1935 which opposed all forced segregation. These were the first instances of the use of the word 'segregation' in church pronouncements and the first official acknowledgement on the part of American Protestantism that the stigmatizing and separating of people on the basis of colour was a proper subject of concern for the churches. The Negro had been terrorized, lynched, starved, segregated in every aspect of life – and this over a period of 70 years during which the churches were supposedly extending their influence in society.

The Social Gospel's direct contribution to the solution of racial difficulties was minimal; in fact, one must say that in its early stages the movement may well have contributed to racial prejudice. One writer has summarized:

. . . The years between Appomattox and Versailles saw the churches almost completely mired on the muddy and rutpocked road to racial equality. Hopkins, May, and the other historians of the rise of social Christianity devote isolated sentences, not chapters or books, to Protestantism's fight for racial justice. The story does not deserve much fuller treatment. Assuredly, the churches contri-

[26] It was the practice of some denominations officially to endorse statements issued by the Federal Council of Churches.

buted alms to the freedmen in the South. They established schools,
hospitals, and charitable institutions to succour the untrained blacks.
But few were the clerical voices to challenge the racial status quo
or to question the divine right superiority of the white man. As
C. Vann Woodward has observed, the quest for social justice in the
early twentieth century, championed so heartily by the churches,
did not embrace justice for the Negro. It is one of the ironies of
American history that the Progressive Era witnessed a retrogression
in the area of race relations. Even as the churches advanced the
Social Gospel, the lines of segregation within the denominations
hardened.[27]

The Theology of the Social Gospel Movement

Let us now look at the theology of the Social Gospel movement to see if there is any clue there as to why a movement
which was primarily concerned with the ethical implications
of the Gospel for society was not concerned with what from
the vantage point of hindsight would have seemed to have
been a very pressing problem indeed. Before looking at specific
doctrines, it may be helpful to look at the general framework
within which these doctrines were elaborated. The most concise
analysis has been made by Toyo-Masa Fuse who found five
doctrinal assumptions underlying the Social Gospel movement:

(1) Social redemption is a prerequisite for individual salvation. Hence the social order must be Christianized.

(2) The main concern of religion must be the establishment
of the Kingdom of God on earth. In this kingdom-building
enterprise man and God are partners.

(3) Progress is immanent and automatic in history.

(4) The power of reason is capable of transcending human
bias and interests. Reason, therefore, is an important instrument
to the understanding of faith and the attainment of progress.

(5) Man is capable of perfecting himself.[28]

27 Robert Moats Miller, *American Protestantism and Social Issues, 1919-1939*
(Chapel Hill, The University of North Carolina Press, 1958), pp. 9-10.
28 Toyo-Masa Fuse, 'The Relevance of Religion in an Age of Conflict: a
case for Dialectical Theology', *Journal of Human Relations*, Vol. 12, No. 2,
1964, pp. 234-235.

Other analysts would disagree only on points of detail with Fuse. Many writers make the point that the Social Gospel movement was much more clear on the type of religion it opposed (religion with an emphasis on sacrament and ritual; religion in which the theological element was of decisive importance; an emotional or mystical type of religion; otherworldly religion, etc.) than on the type of religion it espoused. However, over a period of time certain doctrines came to be fairly clearly defined.

The God of the Social Gospel movement was the God who was understood primarily as the Father of Jesus and as the indwelling spirit of the universe. The early Social Gospel leaders stated quite unequivocally their belief that the sovereignty of God must be interpreted through his Fatherhood. The implications of this belief were very far-reaching as is witnessed to by Rauschenbusch's explanation:

We must democratize the conception of God . . . Jehovah, the keeper of covenants and judge of his people, was changed into the Father in heaven who forgives sins freely, welcomes the prodigal, makes his sun to shine on the just and the unjust, and asks for nothing but love, trust, and co-operative obedience . . . With such a Father spiritual intimacy is possible. With a despotic God prayer is a series of court obeisances and a secret fencing for personal independence. But given such a God as Jesus knew, and the consciousness of him would steal in everywhere and envelop all life in peace . . . Here we see one of the highest redemptive services of Jesus to the human race. When he took God by the hand and called him 'Our Father', he democratized the conception of God . . . He not only saved humanity; he saved God. He gave God his first chance of being loved and of escaping from the worst misunderstandings conceivable.[29]

This is a fairly radical understanding of revelation. Rauschenbusch was not saying merely that the nature of God was to be understood through the perfect revelation of himself in his Son, Jesus Christ − or perhaps this was his intention − but what comes through is a concept of God who possessed the

[29] Walter Rauschenbusch, A Theology for the Social Gospel (New York, The Macmillan Company, 1917), pp. 48, 154, 174.

cardinal human virtues of the time – benevolence, kindness, sympathy and helpfulness.

The other way in which the Social Gospel movement attempted to make God a man of the times was by stressing his immanence. For God to be really benevolent and helpful, he must not be so far separated from man. If 20th century man was too enlightened to swallow the idea that God could understand man because he had become man, what he could swallow was that God was immanent in his own life. Rauschen-busch expressed it this way:

> A God who strives within our striving, who kindles his flame in our intellect, sends the impact of his energy to make our will rest-less for righteousness, floods our subconscious mind with dreams and longings and always urges the race on toward a higher combina-tion of freedom and solidarity – that would be a God with whom democratic and religious men could hold converse as their chief fellow-worker, the source of their energies, the ground of their hopes.[30]

That an extreme doctrine of immanence might degenerate into Pantheism was a danger recognized by a part of the leadership of the Social Gospel movement, but their moderating influence could not quench the spirit of the age or the trend of the ages. As one writer has pointed out, one could see in Puritanism an early indication of a humanizing tendency in American theology which was abetted by its very opponent, revivalism. But in both of these movements or theologies, God was thought of as being in some sense beyond or apart from the world. It was only in the Social Gospel movement that 'a completely ethical human and immanent conception of God is reached and where the typically Biblical elements of the doctrine of God become subordinated.' The God of the Social Gospel is very different from the prophetic God of the Scriptures.[31]

The doctrine of divine immanence had equally far-reaching effects on the Social Gospel doctrine of Christ. Obviously, if carried far enough, it settled the controversy concerning the divinity and humanity of Christ. The divine and human ceased

[30] *Ibid.*, pp. 178-179.
[31] Visser 't Hooft, *op. cit.*, pp. 172-180.

to be alien concepts: 'Everything that is essentially human is included in the nature of God; everything that is essentially divine is found in the nature of man.'[32] Christ, if human, was divine, as are all men. Such an argument by its simplicity cleared the path for what was the real Social Gospel concern – and this was the work of Christ. The Social Gospel, by admission of its leaders, was not really concerned with the metaphysical problems centring around the nature of the person of Christ. In the writings of the movement the strongest accent is always on the teaching rather than on the saving aspect of his mission and on the example of his life rather than on the significance of his death and resurrection. Jesus was seen as the Initiator of the Kingdom of God, and the possibility was open to man to build the Kingdom which Jesus had initiated. Jesus had accomplished his mission because he had achieved an emancipated personality. 'The personality which he achieved was a new type in humanity. Having the power to master and assimilate others, it became the primal cell of a new social organism . . . The personality of Jesus is a call to the emancipation of our own personalities. He has multiplied free souls.'[33] This is pretty curious stuff and is fairly distinctively Rauschenbusch. Other Social Gospel leaders tried to state their doctrine more simply by concentrating on the teaching function of Jesus. Gladden said their theology was 'not, really, very new; it is just as new as the Sermon on the Mount and the Parable of the Prodigal Son, no newer. It is the precise and simple truth which Jesus taught about the Father unburdened of the fictions of mediaeval political science.'[34]

The basic understanding of man in Social Gospel theology was in many ways quite similar to the revivalist understanding. What did change fairly radically was the understanding of sin – and this had indirect consequences for a doctrine of man. The Social Gospel emphasis on divine immanence and earthly progress presupposed a man who had infinite capacities for moral improvement and the capability of full partnership

[32] Gladden, *op. cit.*, p. 137.
[33] Rauschenbusch, *op. cit.*, pp. 152, 162.
[34] Gladden, *op. cit.*, p. 35.

with Jesus in Kingdom-Building. One writer described man
as '. . . but a limited being, but he is an expression of the
divine nature and needs simply to awake to that fact'.[35] Such
a definition obviously required a radical redefinition of salvation as it had been understood by both Puritanism and
revivalism. This in turn might well require a new look at the
concept of sin.

Protestantism has traditionally viewed salvation as involving
some real and fundamental change in man's nature – a dying
to one's self, a putting-on of the 'new man'. Puritanism placed
emphasis on the reliability and measurability of the change;
revivalism placed emphasis on the visibility and abruptness
of the change. Social Gospel theology, however, saw no necessity
for any radical change in man's nature. All that man required
was an awakening to what he really was – a child of God
with infinite possibilities. 'He needs no magical or sacramental
grace but simply the determination, born of his recognition of
his divine sonship to live as a son of God should.'[36] To arrive at
such a conclusion, the Social Gospel movement had to part company decisively with the traditional understanding of sin as
being a power over which man had no control and to which he
was captive. Most of the Social Gospel leadership made the
break with no compunction; a traditional doctrine of original
sin was quite unrealistic and unacceptable to 20th century man.
Sin is 'simply abnormal action. It is the violation, by the soul,
of its own law of life. Whatever tends to the perfection of my
soul, of my manhood, in its physical, intellectual and moral elements, is right. Whatever interferes with that tendency and pre-
vents me from realizing my manhood is wrong.'[37] And 'Sin may
be due simply to imperfect development, racial as well as individual. Man is a product of evolution both in flesh and
spirit . . .'[38] Only Rauschenbusch clung tenaciously to a doctrine of sin, but his basic belief in evolution and progress was so
strong that he was extraordinarily optimistic about the outcome

[35] A. C. MacGiffert, *The Rise of Modern Religious Ideas* (New York, The
Macmillan Company, 1915), p. 206.
[36] *Ibid.*
[37] Gladden, *op. cit.*, p. 66.
[38] MacGiffert, *op. cit.*, p. 184.

of the battle being waged between good and evil. As he saw it, the larger victories had already been won in the evolving human conscience and in the socially conscious western states.

However, the valuable contribution which the Social Gospel movement made to American Protestantism lay in the general area of its doctrine of man. Along with the concepts of evolution and immanence, it attached great importance to the concept of human solidarity. Man was not viewed in the extremely individualistic way which had previously been a mark of both American Protestantism and secularism. Even though the Social Gospel movement provided no Christological or ecclesiological basis for its strong emphasis on the brotherhood of man, its radical departure from individualism was to the good. Mac-Giffert said, 'If there cannot be an isolated personality, or an isolated character, there cannot be isolated salvation. Nobody can be saved *from* society, he must be saved *with* it.'[39] Rauschenbusch announced that he took pleasure in defending the doctrine of original sin because it was 'one of the few attempts of individualistic theology to get a solidaristic view of its field of work.'[40] He was the first American theologian to explore in depth the problem of super-personal forces of evil and to identify 'principalities and power' with groups, institutions, and collective forces in society.

The Social Gospel doctrine of the Church was derived from the negative reaction of its leaders to mysticism and otherworldliness (i.e. the invisible Church) and from their positive understanding of the presence of the Kingdom of God in the world. The Church was defined in instrumental terms – its nature was determined by its function in society. The Church was to serve as a 'training school for the Kingdom', as 'the inspirer and director of social service', as 'the incarnation of the Christ-spirit on earth, the organized conscience of Christendom'. This understanding meant that there was always a conditional

---

[39] *Ibid.*, p. 277. He hereby anticipated Reinhold Niebuhr's position. In an article published in 1963 Niebuhr said '. . . the renewal of the church must certainly include full awareness of the fact that we are all involved in the virtues, the vices, the guilt and the promises of our generation. In a sense it is true that we cannot be saved unless we are all saved.' *The Christian Century*, Vol. LXXX, No. 49, December 4, 1963, p. 1501.

[40] Rauschenbusch, *op. cit.*, p. 50.

(and often negative) quality in the Social Gospel analysis of the Church. The Church was seen as one social institution alongside others – the family, the industrial organization of society, the state. The Kingdom of God was to be found in any or all of these, and it realized itself through any or all of them. Salvation for an individual depended upon his being a part of a community 'which has salvation'. The Church might or might not be that community. 'The saving qualities of the church depend on the question whether it has translated the personal life of Jesus Christ into the social life of its groups and thus brings it to bear on the individual.'[41] If the Church does not meet the test, then it must be 'Christianized' along with other social institutions.

Rauschenbusch was of the opinion that the churches did not generally measure up to the standards which would make them competent for their tasks in the community. He listed four areas in which progress was clearly necessary:

> To become fully Christian the churches must turn their back on dead issues and face their present tasks . . .
> To become fully Christian and to do their duty by society the churches must get together . . .
> To become fully Christian the church must come out of its spiritual isolation . . .
> To become fully Christian the church must still further emancipate itself from the dominating forces of the present era . . .[42]

Research indicates that Rauschenbusch's criticism of the institutional church was justifiable. But neither he nor any Social Gospel leader seemed to understand the Church as anything other than one among a number of social institutions with a primary responsibility for ordering its own house so as to increase its effectiveness. The Baptist minister Philip Moxom's statement, 'There is no sacredness about the church that ought not to be attached to the Chamber of Commerce', is debatable.[43]

One final word must be said about the theological and doctrinal assumptions of the Social Gospel movement. Those who

[41] Rauschenbusch, *op. cit.*, p. 128.
[42] Quoted in Benson Y. Landis, *A Rauschenbusch Reader* (New York, Harper and Bros., 1957), p. 66.
[43] Quoted in Hopkins, *op. cit.*, p. 124.

have studied the movement in any depth agree that its chief concern was with the ethical. Visser 't Hooft, who examined it with great fairness in the attempt to make it more understandable and less repugnant to non-American theologians in the World Council of Churches movement, was forced to the conclusion that in the Social Gospel movement '. . . the ethical is the all-inclusive aspect of Christianity and exhausts its contents'.[44] The anthropocentric trend in American theology was no longer covert. To a much less extent than had the Puritans and revivalists the Social Gospel leaders refused to delude themselves. They openly acknowledged their belief that if Christianity were to work it must not contradict obvious facts. Doctrines which offended modern man's intellect or which were incapable of moving him to pursue the desired goal of the Kingdom of God were either altered or dismissed. Among these were the sovereignty of God, original sin, the incarnation, the atonement, and any concept of the Church as the Body of Christ. The most intelligent analysis of the consequences of this theological 'blackout' to race relations has been made by Will Campbell, a Southern Baptist minister and long-time worker in the field of race relations.[45] Campbell indicates that what really happened in the Social Gospel movement was the culmination of a shift from incarnation to deification – a shift from belief in God-man to man-God. God was no longer understood as having been incarnate in the person of Christ. He did not become man by being 'in Christ'; rather, the man Jesus became God 'as a reward for the life he had lived and the deeds he had performed'. Man was not seen in the light of God's action towards him in Jesus Christ; man really became God. Campbell said at the time of his writing that the ghost of the theology of the Social Gospel movement has largely disappeared but that the ethics of the movement persist. As we shall see, the theological ghost walks again. But his main point was that only when man takes the sovereign God who has revealed himself in Jesus Christ as his point of reference for his understanding

of man is he spared the distortions which come from measuring
other men against himself. Because the Social Gospel's ultimate
concern was with man and society, it could be discriminatory.
Because its ultimate criteria was effectiveness, it could and had
to select the issues with which it would concern itself. This man-
directed theology could result in a 'Brotherhood of Man' expressed in a labour union or a Chamber of Commerce rather
than the Church. Since men did not stand together in all of
their frailty under the judgment of God but stood under man's
judgment, the 'poor negro' was judged, found guilty, and
lynched by the mobs of his peers.

IV

CONTEMPORARY THEOLOGY AND THE NEGRO

If history demands a knowledge of the past but essentially is a living-out of the past in the present; if historical enquiry is an account of 'how we got this way' as an old teacher of mine once put it; that is, if our social heritage, our present belonging to a community, our past-come-alive-in-the-now of our living tradition, all shape us and mould us and make us what we are – then man's memory is no longer a simple 'looking back'; it is a vital and dynamic awareness of the past as it exists in and creates present communal existence and prepares for our future.[1]

The 'live and let live' truce on civil rights which had existed between the southern states and the rest of the United States was finally shattered in the 1940's. What had been the race problem became racial crisis. Once again it was the upheaval of war – this time World War II – which gave impetus to an increasing Negro protest against second-class citizenship. While the war effort benefited the American economy which was still working its way out of depression, the Negro who had suffered the most extreme economic disability had been unable to improve his economic position during the early years of wartime production. In 1941 A. Philip Randolph, president of the Brotherhood of Sleeping Car Porters, began the organization of a march on Washington to protest against discrimination in defence industries. The march did not occur because President Roosevelt signed an executive order forbidding discrimination in defence

---

[1] Norman Pittenger, 'A Contemporary Trend in North American Theology: Process-Thought and Christian Faith', *Religion in Life*, Vol. XXXIV, No. 4, Autumn 1965, p. 505.

industries, defence training programmes, and in Federal Government employment. He also established a President's Committee on Fair Employment Practices to see that the executive order was obeyed. A number of northern states took similar measures to deal with racial discrimination in employment and in some cases went even further by dealing with the policies of public and private employment agencies. There followed a new wave of migration of Negroes to the north and west which broke conclusively the pattern of concentration of Negroes in the rural areas of the south. By the end of the war Negroes had made their first real inroads into semi-skilled and skilled occupations.

It was also in the 1940's that there appeared the first crack in the rigidly-segregated transportation laws. The Supreme Court ruled in 1941 that there must be equality of sleeping car accommodations under the separate but equal principle and ruled again in 1946 against the state of Virginia in a case involving a Negro passenger's refusal to move to the rear of a public vehicle when going into Virginia (which had state laws requiring segregated transportation). In this ruling the Court spoke of the need for a uniform law to protect passengers involved in interstate travel.

World War II served even more than had World War I to add fuel to the fire of discontent of American Negroes. The war could be construed as a war brought about by the racist theories of Hitler, and yet many American soldiers were themselves the victims of racism. An increasing number of white people began to sense the hypocrisy of that situation. Even so, the Armed Forces remained segregated until 1948. But when World War II ended, the resolution of Negroes not to lose the gains they had made was very strong. This resolve, coupled with the increased realization by the Federal Government of the importance of world opinion and abetted by a steadily increasing minority of white liberals, shoved the United States into the crisis and chaos of the 1950's.

During the 1940's the churches' pronouncements concerned with race relations increased greatly in number and moved from the general to the specific. By the end of the decade eight major denominations and the National Council of Churches were on record as opposing segregation in both the Church and society. The pronouncements supported and asked for further government action. They indicated that the churches were becoming aware of the nature of their own problem as segregated institutions. This period also evidenced the first indications that the denominations realized some action was necessary to implement their resolutions. Study commissions were established, and bi-racial committees were appointed to determine appropriate action. However, the churches obviously anticipated a gradual, orderly change and were totally unprepared for the events of the 1950's.

On May 17, 1954, the Supreme Court of the United States opened the gates of the legal prison in which the American Negro had been incarcerated since 1896. Thurgood Marshall, Negro lawyer for the N.A.A.C.P., won his case against public school segregation by unanimous decision of the Supreme Court which ruled that segregated public schools were inherently unequal. The decision 'that to separate (Negro children) from others of similar age and qualifications solely because of their race generates a feeling of inferiority as to their status in the community that may affect their hearts and minds in a way unlikely ever to be undone' had far-reaching ramifications. It could and would be used as a weapon with which to attack any and every form of legalized discrimination in the United States.

A majority of Americans greeted the decision with approbation. Churches welcomed it with prayers of thanksgiving, and Negroes hailed it as the 'final way station' on their long and tortured march towards freedom. But the white south received the word of the decision with shock and unbelief. Although the decision had seemed inevitable in view of previous decisions of the courts, the south was unprepared for what it considered to be the final betrayal. But prepare itself it did. The Supreme Court delayed its finalizing order for one year in order to give segregated school systems an opportunity to plan for desegregation. It was operating on what many people consider to have been the mistaken idea that a gradual transition would result in less severe community disorder. While there was preparation

G

for school desegregation in some of the border states, the preparation was of a quite different kind throughout the deep south. The Ku Klux Klan was reorganized. White Citizens Councils were formed, and their members consisted of responsible and 'respectable' civic and church leaders. The best legal minds of the states were put to work to discover ways by which the ruling could be circumvented. There was no move towards desegregation in the deep south for several years. In the border states the desegregation plans were worked out so as to allow a minimal amount of desegregation while appearing to meet the court requirement of 'deliberate speed' and 'good faith'. It may not be fair to assume that all of the partial plans which placed such a heavy burden on a few Negro children were conceived in malice. But the statements which were made by public officials in defiance of the desegregation ruling make questionable their good intentions.

The first Negro children approached white schools in the south in an atmosphere pregnant with violence and hatred. It became no extraordinary thing to see newspaper photos of a single six-year-old Negro child being led by its parents or a Negro minister through a screaming mob of hundreds of white adults. Schools and churches were bombed; Negro leaders and Negro children were tormented, harassed, and physically assaulted. In town after town there was an absolute breakdown of law and order. This usually resulted in the removal of the Negro children from the newly-desegregated schools in order to prevent further violence by white people. At last the Federal Government was forced to put its weight behind the decision of the courts, and it did so by sending Federal troops to Little Rock, Arkansas, which had become a virtual battleground as a result of the attempt of nine Negro children to enter the public schools of that city. The courage of Negro children, their parents, Negro ministers, and isolated white people who walked with Negroes during those early days of horror in the south is indescribable. In statistical terms the fruit of that heroism was meagre; it has been estimated that some ten years after the decision less than 6% of the Negro children in the southern states were in desegregated schools. But statistics are not the only nor the final measurement of the contribution of such courage.

As has been stated earlier, the churches' response to the 1954 decision was immediate and favourable. The General Board of the National Council of Churches adopted a statement in which it declared that the decision 'gives a clear status in law to a fundamental Christian and American principle'. Every major denomination either at that time or shortly thereafter made pronouncements in which they stressed the essentially Christian character of the decision and called for support and implementation of it by constituent churches. The degree of enthusiasm of the statements ranged from near jubilance to a more reserved note in those of the Southern Baptist Convention and southern Presbyterian church. The four largest Negro denominations – the African Methodist Episcopal, the African Methodist Episcopal Zion, the Colored Methodist Episcopal, and the National Baptist – issued statements commending the Supreme Court for the decision.

The favourable response to the decision which was manifested in denominational pronouncements was not evidenced by congregations at a community level. In the early stages of the desegregation process, these were almost completely silent. There is little evidence to indicate that 'white churches' in local communities took any initiative to produce desegregation or offered assistance in planning prior to desegregation. As desegregation progressed and violence became the pattern, numbers of individual white ministers and laymen took positive action in the face of the violence, sometimes exposing themselves to bodily injury along with Negro ministers, parents, and students. But concerted action usually came in the form of statements by ministerial associations. These statements were very like in tenor the church pronouncements of the 1930's which called for an end to violence and mob action. Their dominant note was a plea for law and order. The most thorough study which has been made of the churches' involvement at a local level in the school desegregation process is Pettigrew and Campbell's study of the Little Rock situation,[2] but there are any number of unpublished

2 Thomas F. Pettigrew and Ernest Q. Campbell, *Christians in Racial Crisis* (Washington, Public Affairs Press, 1959).

studies made by human relations agencies. In almost every instance the conclusion is that the churches by their silence contributed to an atmosphere in which violence was inevitable.

In an attempt to accomplish what pronouncements had not accomplished, the National Council of Churches and a number of denominations deployed staff in the south. The job descriptions of these staff persons differed with the denominations, but in most instances the staff worked primarily within the structures of the churches with an educational approach. Most of the programmes allowed for a minimal amount of co-operative work with other community agencies. These staff persons were often among the early arrivals at scenes of violence and in some cases the only representatives of the 'white church' at the scene. As could be expected, they were resented by local clergymen who considered them to be 'outsiders'.

Another witness of the churches in the 1950's was made by an interdenominational group known as United Church Women. This is a department of the National Council of Churches and is organized on a national, state and local level across the United States. At all of these levels it is the most nearly integrated church group which exists in the states. Both its pronouncements and activity had considerable community impact because of its inter-racial character. The women who devoted their time to this organization were apt to be women who were dissatisfied with the conservatism of their local churches and who were searching for a more adequate mode of expression of their faith.

The second decisive event in the Negroes' new march towards freedom occurred in December of 1955 when Mrs Rosa Parks, a Negro woman, riding a public bus in Montgomery, Alabama, refused to give her seat to a white man. She was arrested, and so the city which was known as the cradle of the Confederacy found itself cradling a movement which would be determinative for the strategy of southern Negroes for the next ten years. From that day on they would no longer place absolute faith in slow-moving court procedures or the goodwill of white people. The Negroes of Montgomery took their struggle into the streets and walked, 50,000 strong, in what was a nearly totally effective bus boycott. The boycott began only as a protest against discourteous treatment, but when the mild requests were met with a refusal to negotiate, harsh treatment, and jailings, they redirected their attack against segregation itself. The N.A.A.C.P. brought court action, and ten months after the boycott began, the Supreme Court upheld a Federal District Court ruling that segregated seating on municipal buses was illegal. Besides the court victory and the example of the possibility of effectiveness of a Negro mass movement and boycott, the Montgomery movement produced an authentic leader of the Negro people. This was Martin Luther King, Jr., a young Baptist minister whose theology had been strongly influenced by his study of Gandhi. From Montgomery King moved on to organize the Southern Christian Leadership Conference to co-ordinate the protest activities of Negro ministers and their congregations throughout the south. The pattern established by the Montgomery movement – non-violent protest as the weapon of mass action followed in due time by court decision – became the pattern of the civil rights struggle.

In 1957 Congress passed a Civil Rights Act which was the first such legislation to be passed by Congress in 80 years. The act was largely directed against the disenfranchisement of Negroes in the southern states. It also established a Commission on Civil Rights with investigating powers. The life of this Commission has been extended by each Congress to the present time, and it also has state counterparts. Each Congress since 1957 has dealt with the question of civil rights, but as the pace of favourable legislative and judicial activity has increased, so has increased the Negroes' impatience. Most especially during the late 1950's it seemed that each war won in Washington only freed the Negro to fight more battles at home against an opposition who out-numbered, out-powered, and out-moneyed him. The 1950's ended with continued violence which was cutting ever deeper into the raw nerves of the Negro people.

A new phase of the Negro revolt was initiated in February of 1960 by four Negro college students in Greensboro, North Carolina. They requested service at an all-white lunch counter in a local Woolworth's store, and when they were refused, they remained seated at the counter. Within hours Negro students all across the south began to seat themselves at drug and dime store lunch counters. As the movement gained momentum and it became apparent that the reaction against it would lead to violence, workshops on non-violence were set up by the Congress on Racial Equality and the N.A.A.C.P. But the leadership for the demonstrations remained local and in the hands of the students. Negro students were joined by white students in many cities where there were both white and Negro colleges. The 'sit-ins' were staged in more than a hundred cities, and nearly 4,000 students and supporters were arrested before the sit-ins came to a halt. Students in the north participated in the movement by raising money for bail and by picketing northern branches of the chain stores which were discriminating in the south. Out of this phase of the student movement there grew the extension of the use of the economic boycott. In a number of cities the adult Negro community reinforced the demands of the militant Negro students by withdrawing their patronage from the stores being demonstrated against. In some instances they were joined in the boycott by liberal white persons. As could have been anticipated, the student movement did not confine itself to the desegregation of lunch counters. The movement was not a mere protest against one of the manifestations of prejudice, but was a protest against segregation itself and was rooted in the same deep dissatisfaction and unrest which pervaded the entire Negro community. The youthfulness and enthusiasm of the students had led them to discover a form of protest which was particularly effective and appealing. In the next two years they ran the gamut of 'ins', – sit-ins, read-ins (public libraries), stand-ins (cinemas and theatres), wade-ins (beaches and swimming pools), and kneel-ins (churches). Of these the least effective and short-lived were the kneel-ins due in part to the students' acknowledged indifference as to whether or not they gained admission to 'white churches'. During this period of intense activity the students organized themselves into the Student Non-Violent Coordinating Committee, and in due course they turned their attention to such activities as voter registration programmes in the deep south and tutorial programmes for Negro children in both north and south.

There was a period of extreme violence in the late spring and early summer of 1961 when the Congress of Racial Equality decided to test racial discrimination in interstate travel terminals in the south. Bi-racial teams rode buses across the south and were attacked by mobs and jailed on charges of disturbing the peace. Buses were overturned and burned. More than a thousand persons, including a number of white clergymen, participated in the rides. The legal decision as to the unconstitutionality of segregation in interstate travel had already been made, so the purpose of the Freedom rides was to demonstrate the lack of compliance with the law in the south. This purpose was fully accomplished. As violence mounted, the Interstate Commerce Commission issued a ruling which required that signs requiring desegregated seating be posted in interstate carriers and which forbade the usage of segregated terminals by interstate carriers. Once again pressure resulting in violence led to clarification of the law and a move towards law obedience by southern cities.

In an attempt to focus clearly the full implications of the direct action movement as it had manifested itself in boycotts, the sit-ins, Freedom Rides, and other demonstrations (and there had been some notable failures), the Southern Christian Leadership Conference chose Birmingham, Alabama, as its target city for the spring of 1963. During five weeks of demonstrations there was violence and brutality of a nature which shocked a nation which thought it had grown accustomed to violence. Police dogs and high pressure fire hoses were loosed on Negro children. The headquarters and homes of Negro civil rights leaders were bombed. Angry Negro mobs burst into the streets. For a few hours before the rioting areas of the city were sealed off, the nation was given its first glimpse of a civil rights struggle where non-violence was no longer the technique of the minority. Peace of a sort was finally reached, but the mood of Birmingham spread across the south. The Justice Department reported 758 demonstrations in 186 cities in the ten weeks following the Birmingham riot.

At this point, it may be well to glance back at white participation in the struggle during the early 1960's. There had been limited participation by white people in each of the forms the direct action programme took, but with the exception of the student movement white persons were in a very small minority. White participation was on an individual basis, and in the case of the largest group, the students, there was no claim to religious motivation. Despite the mass movement's philosophy of non-violence, it engendered extreme violence from those who opposed it. The churches were on record as opposing violence. They were in a difficult position concerning the student movement's weapon of civil disobedience because former pronouncements had emphasized obedience to the law. So the major denominations spent the greater part of their time in the early '60's trying to work their way out of the philosophical cul-de-sac into which they had manoeuvred themselves.

In January of 1963 it looked as though the denominations might have recovered (or perhaps discovered) their bearings, for they reached a definite turning point in their strategy in race relations. A conference was assembled at a national level under the aegis of Protestantism, Roman Catholicism, and Judaism, the stated purposes of which were to commemorate the centennial of the Emancipation Proclamation, to examine the role of religious institutions in race relations, and to propose and inspire renewed action. Six hundred and fifty-seven delegates met in Chicago[3] and spent several days addressing themselves to the failure of religion in the national crisis of race relations. The conference was widely praised and widely criticized by those who were in attendance and those who were not. One of the speakers on the opening day denounced it as being 'too little, too late, and too lily-white'. *Time* magazine wrote of it: 'The Churches of the United States, which

---

[3] Ironically, the meeting place was one of the more fashionable Chicago hotels. The Negro taxi driver who took me there from the Airport commented on the number of trips he had made there that day and asked what kind of convention was being held. When I answered that it was a conference on race relations, he laughed and said, 'Well, honey, you be sure and let us know down town what you all decide.'

have never summoned enough resolution, originality, or unity
to help the country significantly in dealing with racial discrimination, last week in Chicago held their first National Conference on Religion and Race, and proved themselves still
unable to offer much wisdom.'4 Much of the criticism was
well-founded, but the fact remained that the spring and summer of 1963 produced an unparalleled burst of activity on the
part of the churches. The National Council of Churches and
most denominations appointed committees on race relations
to which they allocated substantial sums of money and a part
of whose purpose was to involve the churches in direct action.
White churchmen now marched with the official blessings of
their denominations. The most visible demonstration of the
new spirit of the churches was their participation in the March
on Washington on August 28, 1963, when 200,000 citizens con-
verged on the Capitol to demonstrate their determination that
full citizenship rights be achieved for all citizens of the United
States. Churchmen were also given substantial credit for the
passage of the Civil Rights Act of 1964 which was a very strong
bill. It covered equal access to all public accommodation, prohibited discrimination in any state programme receiving
Federal aid, outlawed racial barriers in employment, in labour
union membership, and in voting; and authorized the Justice
Department to bring suits for desegregation of public schools.
The churches also provided strong support for the passage of
the Voting Act of 1965 which made more effective previous civil
rights legislation concerned with voting. With the passage of this
Act one could say that Jim Crow as a legal entity was dead.
Throughout this period representatives of the hierarchy of the
denominations were in the forefront of direct action movements
such as the march in Selma, Alabama, to urge passage of the
Voting Act and voter registration projects in Mississippi. Participation was not without cost, and white persons died along
with Negroes for their cause.

When the denominations embarked on their direct action
programme, any number of people both within and without
the churches raised basic questions concerning motivation

4 *Time*, January 25, 1963.

which implied the further question of the perseverance of the
churches.[5] The churches were accused by some of their own
members of 'me-tooism' – of coming into the battle only when
the government and Negro groups had made it clear which
was the winning side. One churchman wrote:

> In brief, the sudden excitement in the churches and within the
> leadership of the churches over the racial crisis seems to arise from
> an anxiety over the survival of white ascendancy in the churches
> and in the leadership of the churches rather than from either com-
> passion for the people of colour or passion for the gospel which is
> the means by which all people may dwell in reconciliation.[6]

And another churchman warned:

> Unless we can say, 'We are not pagans, this is the way we believe
> because we are in this household of faith, this is what it means to be
> a Jew, this is what it means to be a Christian, this is how we
> behave because of what we believe' – unless this can be said then I
> am convinced that all our techniques, all our gimmicks, pro-
> gram kits and human engineering will fail . . . We must under-
> stand that our actions must be based, not on what we may be able
> to accomplish, but on the basis of what we are, and on the basis
> of our very nature.[7]

A bit earlier a general word of warning had been issued to
the nation – a word which it was very difficult for those who
were involved in marches and demonstrations and who were
making some progress to hear. As early as 1962 Harold Isaacs
spoke prophetic words:

> Victory comes in sight, but it comes late and it comes slowly. It
> comes, moreover, not because the democratic creed, much less the
> Christian, is triumphing at last but because the white world is
> forced to change its ways out of fear for itself. I remember the late
> Franklin Frazier, a few weeks after the 1954 school decision, putting
> it in his own bald and bitter way – I edit only slightly: 'The white
> man is scared down to his bowels, so it's be-kind-to-Negroes-decade
> at last.' The victory approaches so late, and for so many 'wrong

[5] See footnote 7, page 11.

[6] William Stringfellow, *Free in Obedience* (New York, The Seabury Press,
1964), p. 80.

[7] Will D. Campbell, *Race: Challenge to Religion*, editor, Mathew Ahmann
(Henry Regnery Company, Chicago, 1963), p. 20.

reasons' that for many it begins to bear the visage of defeat. More, it comes here and not there, for some but not for others, enough to end forever the old submission but not enough to assure a new freedom . . . The longer the process stretches out, the more stubborn the resistance within pockets of the white society, the more the issue gets wrapped up in the nation's embattlement for survival as a power in the world, the greater the disarray and disorientation, the greater the cynicism rising hard and ugly, especially among young Negroes who emerge to find the fruit of the struggle rotten.[8]

Negroes in the northern ghettoes began to declare the rottenness of the fruit in the summer of 1964. The major battles in civil rights had been waged in the south and against legalized segregation, and those voices which had warned that the war had to do with *de facto* segregation in the north and the larger issue of humanity had gone unheard. In the early '60's for the first time in American history a majority of Negro Americans lived outside the old Confederate states. The minority who had moved out of the south earlier had discovered that the whites had more subtle ways than legislation to keep the Negro in 'his place'. So the Negro in the north must have watched the struggle of the Negro in the south with mixed feelings. On the one hand, he must have admired his southern brother who seemed to have the white man on the run. On the other hand, his own experience would make him doubt that the white man could ever really be put on the run. School segregation outside the south was increasing as residential segregation increased. The rate of unemployment among Negroes was twice as high as that of whites. The gap between the median income of white and Negro workers was widening rather than narrowing. Civil rights legislation had simply failed to touch the problems of Negroes who were trapped in the ghettoes of America's cities – trapped not by legislation, but by a history of overt and covert oppression by white people who would have denied racial prejudice and who had been vocal in their condemnation of the segregated south.

Harlem was the first ghetto to burst into flame, and it was followed by Rochester, Jersey City, Chicago and Philadelphia.

[8] Harold R. Isaacs, 'Integration and the Negro Mood', *Commentary*, December, 1962 (Reprint).

The year 1964 was an election year, and civil rights leaders pleaded for an end to rioting and a moratorium on demonstrations which might provoke violence until President Lyndon Johnson was safely elected. The Negro community responded and rallied round Johnson, who after his election pushed through Congress the already-mentioned Voting Act of 1965. Five days after its passage, Watts, a Negro district of Los Angeles, California, exploded into the worst riot in American history. The 1964 riots which were spread across the north cost eight lives and over 1,000 injuries. Watts alone cost 34 lives and another 1,000 injuries. In 1967 there was a decrease in the number of deaths and injuries but a large increase in the number and distribution of riots which for the first time moved into the south. The long, hot summer of 1967 produced riots in 20 cities with a death toll of over 74 and more than 2,000 injuries. By the end of that summer persons high in government circles were being quoted as saying that the United States was close to a new civil war. A Senate investigation committee quoted figures for the three years 1965-67: more than 100 riots in 76 cities, 130 deaths, 3,623 injured, 7,985 cases of arson, 28,932 arrests, 5,434 convictions, property damage of $216 million, and other economic loss, $504 million.

Any number of factors had operated to arouse the ghettoes from their sullen sleep. The 'be-kind-to-Negroes-decade' to which Franklin Frazier made reference in 1954 was drawing to a close in 1964. The call for a moratorium on demonstrations in 1964 was politically expedient, but it symbolized the continuing necessity for the Negro to adjust his expectations to the white man's timetable. Consensus among white people was that Negroes were trying to move too fast, and there had been predictions that a white backlash was developing which might influence the 1964 elections. The fact that it did not do so made the prediction and the assumptions underlying it no less repugnant to Negroes. A white backlash could only mean that the majority group still denied the rights and humanity of the minority group. Negroes denied that the white backlash was a new reaction to their gains or to the rate of their progress and contended that it was the exposure of dormant prejudice which had always existed among white people in the northern and western states. The white reaction to the early riots was one of fear and incomprehension. There were frantic calls for more repressive police action and for federal laws to control rioting. The attempt to pass effective civil rights legislation in 1966 dealing with segregation in housing failed, and there had not been the all-out effort for its passage by either the President or church groups as in previous years. The incomprehension of white people was made painfully clear by their belief that repressive measures would be an effective deterrent to ghetto riots. The inhabitants of the ghettoes were quite accustomed to police brutality and violence; for the first time, however, they were at least partially on the giving as well as the receiving side.

The decision to discuss the white backlash before discussing the black power movement is a deliberate one indicating agreement with the view that black violence is a reaction to the white community's still massive and monolithic prejudice, stupidity, and intransigence. This may seem a harsh indictment in the face of the civil rights legislation which has been passed by a largely white Congress, but it must be remembered that in every instance the legislation was opposed by those white persons whom it most directly affected. And the will to enforce the legislation has been very weak. The rising expectations of Negroes have shattered themselves against the hard facts of reality – that the richest nation in the world which spends billions of dollars annually to help the poor in other countries, and to wage war, either cannot or will not spend the sums necessary to salvage the lives of its own poor and oppressed. As one Negro said: 'We have marched, we have cried, we have prayed, we have voted, we have petitioned, we have been good little boys and girls. We have done every possible thing to make this white man recognize us as human beings, and he refuses . . .' and therefore, 'We are going to fight your people like you fight us.'

The slogan 'Black Power' was first shouted in Mississippi in 1966 by Stokeley Carmichael, a leader of S.N.C.C. His shout marked the beginning of a deep rift in what had been a solid

civil rights movement. The leading civil rights organizations –
the N.A.A.C.P., the Urban League, C.O.R.E., S.C.L.C. and
S.N.C.C. – had in the past sometimes disagreed on matters
of tactics, timing or techniques, but there had been general
agreement that their goal was integration and that it could best
be reached by adherence to the principle of non-violence. Martin
Luther King had maintained his position as leader and spokes-
man of the Negro people for nearly a decade during which
time he had been named 'Man of the Year' by *Time* magazine
and awarded the Nobel peace prize.

From the beginning of the 1930's there had been a small
and fragmented black nationalist movement growing in the
cities. The strongest and best-organized of the groups which
composed this movement were the Black Muslims whose membership in 1962 was estimated at anywhere between 100,000 and
250,000. Very little significance had been attached to this group
by white people or by the majority of Negroes in the civil
rights movement because their philosophy and programme
seemed to express quite the opposite of the desires of the
majority of Negroes. This form of black nationalism as it was
described in 1962 seemed quite remote from the reality of that
day :

The Muslims represent the current most extreme form of want-
ing *out*, out of America, out of the white world altogether. They
recruit their members from among the lowly with a doctrine that
declares the white man to be the devil himself doomed for his evil
deeds. They demand total separation for themselves, asking for land
to be carved out of the territory of the United States on which they
would make a fresh start as the nation of black men chosen by God
to embody virtue on earth. The Muslims call on the Negro American to cease being both 'Negro' and 'American'. They reject the
term 'Negro' as the badge of subjection and seek to rid themselves
of everything else that has come to them out of the white man's
culture including not only the names acquired out of slavery, but
many of the more bitter fruits of degradation and poverty . . . They
acquire new habits of life, a new view of themselves and of their
blackness, a new kind of militant self-respect which many other
Negroes look upon with fascinated envy. Like Marcus Garvey,
Muhammad appeals essentially to racial pride and separateness.
His passionately violent indictment of the white world carries the

ring of truth to almost any listening Negro, and his defiant rejection
of the white society brings an involuntary inward asserting response
from many otherwise not at all ready to accept the melancholy
suggestion that their road to recognition lies in black racism and
in a total flight from social reality.[9]

These words which seemed in 1962 to be a description of a
fanatic, lunatic fringe seem in 1968 to be a reasoned account
of the feelings of a vast number of American Negroes.

It is questionable whether American Negroes have officially
joined the Black Muslim movement in great numbers. Rather,
they have adopted and adapted parts of its philosophy and have
produced a much wider and more diverse form of black
nationalism. The person who was most instrumental in dis-
seminating the new gospel of white hatred and black pride
was Malcolm X, minister of the New York City Temple of
Black Muslims. His commitment seems to have been firmly
religious, but he was forced out of the Black Muslim movement,
or so he claimed, after an intemperate speech concerning
President Kennedy's assassination. The following which he
had acquired remained faithful to him and continued to grow.
While his excoriation of the white man was an essential part
of his appeal to the dispossessed of the ghettoes, Malcolm X's
leadership was very much the result of a great personal charisma
and the fact that he was willing to confront on its own terms
and in its own language a white society dominated by hate.
What he said was not as important as the fact that he said it.
His apotheosis was completed by his death. Although three
Black Muslims were convicted of his murder, he is to thousands
in the ghettoes the Shining Black Prince who was destroyed by the white devils. These thousands glimpsed in Carmichael's shout in Mississippi a resurrection of their dead
leader's dreams.

The white community and much of the civil rights establishment moved swiftly to denounce Carmichael – the white community on the ground that he was inciting violence, and the
civil rights establishment on the ground that a black power
movement which implied black separation could only be self-

[9] Isaacs, *op. cit.*

defeating. The fact seems to be that Carmichael himself had
not attempted to formalize the implications of his slogan but
that it represented his own belief that Negroes must develop
a racial pride which could only come as a result of a black
economic and political power base. He had reached this conclusion after working in voter registration drives in the deep
south. Several months after the Mississippi episode Carmichael
and the staff of S.N.C.C. set about the preparation of a position
paper on the meaning of black power. That it was S.N.C.C.
which gave birth to a new philosophy which is interpreted by
many to be black racism is ironic, for this was the organization
which had seemed for a time to be a shining example of integration. One can only speculate as to the nature of the internal
tension which combined with external events to convert the
Student Non-Violent Coordinating Committee into what is
now essentially a black separatist group led by Rap Brown,
who openly advocates violence. Carmichael was less inflamma-
tory than Brown and was able even in the initial stages of
discussion to carry with him C.O.R.E. which had also acquired
new militant leadership in 1966. Both the N.A.A.C.P. and the
Urban League stood in direct opposition to the black power
movement. Martin Luther King as leader of the S.C.L.C. and
as the still-acknowledged spiritual leader of American Negroes
in 1966 chose for himself the role of mediator between the
openly-split civil rights groups.

The black power movement might have destroyed itself (and
may yet), but it had working for it in 1966 and 1967 the one
force which was essential for its survival and the one force
which was able to heal the division among the civil rights
organizations – a very nearly unqualified, monolithic white
opposition. The emasculated Civil Rights bill of 1966 was
followed in 1967 by an Anti-Riot Act and by a reduction in
government expenditures on programmes aimed at alleviating
the conditions which committee after committee had testified
produced riots. Perhaps the final straw came when the House
of Representatives not only refused to consider but made a
joke of a bill to appropriate funds to rid city slums of rats which
testimony had indicated bit, sometimes fatally, at least 14,000

people a year. That the bill was passed by a shame-faced Congress at a later session in no way lessened the initial insult to the ghetto dwellers. Such actions and attitudes in the white community, plus a growing realization on the part of civil rights organizations that they were not in touch with the masses of people, have led to the development of a new mood among Negro Americans – which can be described variously as black power, black pride, or black consciousness.

No consensus has been reached either as to definition or programme in this new phase of the Negro's fight for freedom. Those who find themselves united behind a general idea of 'black is good' range through the 'do-rag nationalists' – angry street-corner kids with their processed hair done up in black rags – Carmichael and Brown who have established ties with black nationalists around the world, the established organizations who now maintain that pride in race has always been one of their goals, and the newly-formed National Committee of Negro Churchmen. The tactics these groups would advocate would vary from guerrilla warfare and armed rebellion to a continuation of programmes aimed at integration but on the black man's terms and with his timetable. The diversity is so great as to make the unity precarious, but on one point there is firm unity – opposition to all those who ignore or take lightly the significance of this growing black pride and consciousness.

The attempt to deal with the rightful indictment of American society and the just claims which the Negro makes against it with white repressive power is an indication of tragic ignorance. This is, after all, the unsuccessful policy followed by the United States for these hundreds of years. It is little wonder that there is once again talk among Negroes of their extermination and that they prophesy that the ghettoes will become concentration camps. It is equal ignorance to attempt to locate the cause of Negro rebellion in outside forces. Negroes whose unemployment rate is twice as high as whites' and whose median income is only half as much as whites' do not need to be told by Communists that their society has failed them. It is surely the wrong moment in history to confront black power and black pride with white power and white pride. As blacks

H

and whites arm themselves, the silence of the churches speaks
loudly.

Contemporary Theology

We have examined the record of the churches in the contemporary period and have seen that they became increasingly
vocal in their pronouncements against segregation and for a few
years joined in an active and militant campaign against it. However, we stand too close to the contemporary scene to analyse
its theology in terms of movements. It was Sydney Ahlstrom,
I believe, who said that an interpretation of the present
requires a seer rather than a historian. As was indicated in
the first chapter, reputable historians have found the three
movements which have been discussed to be formative of
American Protestantism and have contended that a synthesis
of Puritanism, revivalism, and the Social Gospel is the dominant
theology of American Protestantism today. However, there
have been some new emphases in theology in the United States
during the period under consideration which may have influenced the churches to a measurable degree, and these must
be examined briefly.

Prior to this, a few words must be said about the so-called
'Negro churches'. A tremendous amount of claptrap has been
spoken and written about the religion of American Negroes.
The widespread belief that the character of the religion practised by Negroes is an absolute derivative of the character
and culture of American Negroes is very suspect indeed. It
is true that the 'Negro church' offered itself as a safety valve
or escape hatch for the sadness and joy of a whole people who
were not allowed to participate in American society or culture.
It is also true that the 'Negro church' has served as a training
school for eventual participation in society and as an effective
social agency. What is questionable is whether these characteristics are essentially characteristics of 'Negro' institutions. Negro
'churches' and denominations came into existence during the
period when revivalism was the shaping movement of Protestantism, and the emotionalism which is generally considered

to be a feature of Negro denominations is hardly less pronounced in many Methodist and Baptist churches and sect
groups which have white membership of corresponding economic and social status. Revivalism and the Social Gospel movement in the late 19th century combined to turn any number
of churches (with white membership) into social service agencies
– in particular when there were no existing agencies to deal with
community problems. Much of the analysis of 'Negro churches'
has been made by white persons outside the churches. What
seems to be true is that 'Negro churches' and denominations are
subject to very much the same class stratifications to which
'white churches' and denominations are subject and this has had
an effect on the form of worship (and the theological under-
girding of worship) in both instances. It has in both instances
affected the involvement of the churches with their communities. It is for this reason that no particular attempt was
made to differentiate between the activity of 'white' and
'Negro' churches in this study until the contemporary period
was reached. Prior to that time, quiescence is the word most
descriptive of the institutional church's stance in the matter of
race relations regardless of the colour of membership. The
'Negro church' began its activity during the contemporary
period earlier than the 'white church' and has sustained its
activity for a longer period.

The new strands in contemporary theology which must be
examined briefly are dialectical theology, neo-orthodoxy,
relational theology, and radical Christianity. It is impossible
to do more than look at each and see how it is related to the
general theological tenor of American Protestantism and the
extent to which it may be expected to affect the churches' involvement in the problems of race relations.

Dialectical Theology

Dialectical theology is the name given to the theology of
Reinhold Niebuhr, who probably has been the single most
influential American theologian of the 20th century. One cannot say that a school developed around his theology – indeed

he contended he was not a theologian – but his influence spread through his students, his writings, and his involvement in civic life. He has been categorized by some as being the representative of an enlightened Social Gospel movement and by others as being a part of the neo-orthodox movement. It would be difficult to justify placing his theology in either of these categories without investigating it exhaustively, so it will be considered separately.

Niebuhr was reared in the tradition of conservative Lutheran and Reformed theology but became vitally interested in the social witness of Christianity while serving as pastor of a congregation of factory workers in Detroit. However, he was unable to accept the Social Gospel premise that society as a whole was capable of transformation or 'Christianization', as Rauschenbusch put it. He contended that the discontinuity between individual and social morality was much more radical than the Social Gospel leaders thought and that society more naturally expressed the original sin of self-interest and pride than did individuals. His conclusion was that the ethic of Jesus stood in judgment over every ethical situation and that there-fore while the Christian worked for every possible reform, he could never expect to attain the 'absolute good'.[10] Niebuhr is credited with having split asunder the too-simple world view of the early Social Gospel movement without deserting its basic concern with the social situation and man's participation in it.

The point at which Niebuhr broke radically with the Social Gospel was in his understanding of the nature of man and sin. He felt that the prevailing view of man in Western culture was derived from the commingling of the classical and Biblical traditions which resulted in an over-emphasis on human virtue and intelligence, whereas '. . . the Christian view of human nature is involved in the paradox of claiming a higher stature for man and of taking a more serious view of his evil than other anthropology'.[11] What he was concerned to establish was that

---

[10] Paul Allan Carter, *The Decline and Revival of the Social Gospel* (Ithaca, Cornell University Press, 1956), pp. 154 ff.

[11] Reinhold Niebuhr, *The Nature and Destiny of Man*, Volume I (London, Nisbet & Co. Ltd., 1941), p. 18.

'both the majesty and the tragedy of human life exceed the dimension within which modern culture seeks to comprehend human existence'.[12]

Niebuhr contended that the occasion for man's sin is the ambiguity of his position as he stands in and yet above nature. Man's involvement in natural contingencies makes him insecure; he attempts to overcome his insecurity by a will-to-power which overreaches the limits of his creatureliness. Man has the limitations of a finite mind; his pretence that he is not thus limited infects all of his intellectual pursuits with the sin of pride. His will-of-power and his pride disturb the harmony of creation. Sin manifests itself in both 'religious and moral terms' – the religious dimension being man's rebellion against God and his effort to usurp the place of God, and the social dimension being injustice or the subordination of other life to his own will.[13] Group pride is merely an aspect of the pride and arrogance of individuals, but it is more pernicious because the claims of a collective self exceed those of the individual ego and because group pride achieves a certain authority over the individual. Even this brief exposition of Niebuhr's doctrine of sin indicates the impossibility of his remaining in line with the older Social Gospel belief in man's abilities and potentialities. His doctrine of sin demanded a Christ who not only disclosed the true meaning of life but who made available the resources to fulfil that meaning.

It was Niebuhr's doctrine of man and his understanding of justification which laid the foundations for his social ethics. The understanding of human nature determines the limits of what should be attempted in society as well as the direction of ethical action. The limits are themselves a form of direction in that they steer one away from the effort to find absolute solutions and lead one towards 'proximate' solutions. The doctrine of justification (which Niebuhr understood to mean that divine mercy imputes the perfection of Christ to the converted self and accepts its intentions for achievements) frees a Christian to act in a sinful world 'to do the next best thing even though

---

[12] *Ibid.*, p. 130.   [13] *Ibid.*, p. 191.

it involves participation in the corporate evil which produces real conflicts of conscience'.[14]

When one turns to the specific question of race relations, one finds that Niebuhr spoke of it fairly infrequently. However, in his very early writing in the 1930's, he discussed the applicability of the technique of non-violence to the situation of the American Negro and pointed out that this was a possible middle course between hopeless reliance on the power of education or moral persuasion to change the white man and the equally hopeless choice of violent revolution by the Negro.[15] King's later adoption of non-violence was not on the basis of its being a technique which was all Niebuhr's ethic would allow it to be, and Niebuhr questioned fairly sharply King's definition of the non-violence movement as the way of love. Still another early but indirect contribution which Niebuhr made to race relations was through his students in the south who organized the Fellowship of Southern Churchmen, the forerunner of the Committee of Southern Churchmen, to which reference will be made later. In 1938 the Fellowship was able to get the signatures of fifty prominent southerners on a manifesto calling for full citizenship rights for all people, and this manifesto was published in papers across the country.

Niebuhr's system of proximate solutions is well-illustrated by his reaction to the 1954 Supreme Court decision. He first stated that the 'separate but equal' decision of 1806 was a 'very good doctrine for its day' in that the 1954 decision at the beginning of the century would have prompted revolt – 'and revolt which is so widespread that police cannot suppress it represents defeat both of the law and ideal'. In speaking of the 1954 decision in its own time, he said

. . . an organic and slowly developing progress towards justice appears for the present to have been thwarted by a decision which spelled out the ultimate goal of the process. The explicit challenge of the moral standard seems to have aroused subconscious fears and

14 Charles W. Kegley, and Robert W. Bretall, Editors, *The Library of Living Theology, Volume II, Reinhold Niebuhr, His Religious, Social, and Political Thought* (New York, The Macmillan Company, 1956), p. 50.

15 Reinhold Niebuhr, *Moral Man and Immoral Society* (London, SCM Press, 1963), pp. 252-254.

prejudices which might have been gradually beguiled by a slower approach to the ultimate standard.[16]

Needless to say, many supporters of racial justice would take severe issue with Niebuhr at that point.

The doctrine which has not been examined which may have some bearing on the question of Niebuhr's influence on Protestantism and race relations is his doctrine of the Church. It is there that Niebuhr seemed least able to escape the Social Gospel mentality, and it is there that he is most generally criticized. Charles West, one of his students, said:

> . . . On the whole Niebuhr's criticisms of the Church far outweigh his constructive statements about its vocation. The Church as a free community in an unfree society, as a source of truth and love where these are officially distorted, as a point of contact between the power of God and the powerless Christian giving him direction and strength in his witness – these are themes which Niebuhr has not developed, for he remains too much the Christian-in-society to appreciate their full value.[17]

Unlike the Social Gospel theologians, Niebuhr did not view the Church in instrumental terms, but like them, he was chary of seeing the Church as the Body of Christ, the redeemed community whose redemption depended not at all upon itself. Actually, Niebuhr spoke very little of the Church at all, but when he did, it was more in terms of ideal than fact. In one instance he spoke of it rather differently and this in connection with race relations:

> Nothing can hide the fact that this religiously sanctified racial parochialism has been a grievous offense against the very ideals of the Christian faith. But it has also been the negative by-product of one of the genuine achievements of the sectarian church in our nation: the creation of integral communities on the level of local congregations. This actual 'chumminess' of the local congregation has invalidated the universal principle at the heart of the Gospel. Particular brotherhood, ethnically based, has invalidated the universal brotherhood implicit in the Christian ethic.[18]

[16] Harry R. Davis and Robert C. Good, *Reinhold Niebuhr on Politics* (New York, Charles Scribner's, Sons 1960), pp. 228-232.

[17] Charles C. West, *Communism and the Theologians* (Philadelphia, The Westminster Press, and London, SCM Press, 1958), p. 175.

[18] Davis and Good, *op. cit.*, p. 235.

Although Niebuhr was fundamentally concerned with man in society, his doctrines of Christ and sin saved him from the overwhelming anthropocentricism of much of American theology. However, his inability to produce a doctrine of the Church may have lessened the impact his theology could have made in the area of race relations. This inability may have been the result of the nature of dialectical theology with its scepticism of any absolute, which led to an under-emphasis on the completed work of Christ.

Neo-Orthodoxy

The influence of Continental theologians began to make itself felt in the United States in the late 1930's. American theologians were involved in the ecumenical movement, and increasing numbers of seminary students were studying abroad. Niebuhr had loosed his attack against liberalism and the Social Gospel movement. As early as 1945 Paul Lehmann said that neo-orthodoxy was the decisive intellectual force in the contemporary Protestant church.[19] And another writer said that by 1949 it was difficult to find a current book on theology which did not defend the position of neo-orthodoxy.[20]

Neo-orthodoxy is the very broad term used in the United States to categorize the theology influenced by the 'new-Reformation' and the existentialist emphasis of Continental theologians. The most representative of the former was Karl Barth and of the latter Paul Tillich. These men were poles apart on much of their doctrine, but what emerged in the United States as a result of their influence was an emphasis on some major themes which were common to Continental theology: a reassertion of the sovereignty of God; a reaction against an optimistic evaluation of the human situation; a new appreciation of the centrality of biblical revelation; a revival of interest in Christology; a deepening concern to recover a sense of wholeness in the life of the Church; and a tendency among the

[19] Paul Lehmann, 'The Rebirth of Theology', *Religion in Life*, Vol. XIV, No. 4, Autumn 1945, p. 583.
[20] Waymon Parsons, 'The Theological Pendulum', *Religion in Life*, Vol. XVIII, No. 4, Autumn 1949, p. 567.

leaders of the theological revival to move to the 'left' politically while moving to the 'right' theologically.

It is difficult to assess the depth to which neo-orthodoxy penetrated the lives of the churches. Certainly most seminary students in the late '40's and early '50's were exposed to this theology. There was a movement towards serious theological enquiry by lay groups in some local congregations in the 1950's, and several denominations were using the Presbyterian U.S.A. curriculum material (which was based on neo-orthodox theology) in their church schools. But the 'return to religion' in the United States in the 1950's seemed to have little relation to the theological revival. Bennett described the two as being nearly antithetical and contended that the religious revival played down the distinctively Christian and was used to give religious sanction to culture.[21]

It is clear that the premises of neo-orthodoxy were incompatible with the mentality of the average 20th century American of whom one writer has said:

(he) was still optimistic, still took for granted that his was the most favoured of all countries, the happiest and most virtuous of all societies, and, though less sure of progress, was still confident that the best was yet to be. Two world wars had not induced in him either a sense of sin or that awareness of evil almost instinctive with most Old World peoples . . .[22]

This point was illustrated by the criticism which Sweet, a religious historian, made of Barth's theology:

This boils down to mean that man and God cannot work together to make a better world. It means the absolute rejection of the entire Social Gospel emphasis; that God alone can reform society; but God is not interested in society. His concern is to attend and assist the individual soul 'in its passage through time to eternity' . . . Here is quietism *par excellence*; a do-nothing theology, which to the average American seems to be perfect nonsense.[23]

---

[21] John C. Bennett, *Christianity and Crisis*, Vol. XVI, No. 16, October 1, 1956.

[22] Henry Steele Commager, *The American Mind* (New Haven, Yale University Press, 1950), pp. 409-410.

[23] William Warren Sweet, *The American Churches, An Interpretation* (London, The Epworth Press, 1947), p. 69.

Professor Sweet stated (no matter how limited his understanding of Barth) the major criticism which American Protestantism brought to bear against neo-orthodoxy – that it was
not conducive to social action. Prominent American theologians – Paul Tillich, the Niebuhrs, Paul Lehmann, John
Bennett, and Paul Ramsey – were all forced to give serious consideration to Continental theology. But by 1960 there would
probably have been general agreement in theological circles
with Reinhold Niebuhr who said that Barth's theology was
'irrelevant to all Christians in the Western World who believe
in accepting common and collective problems without illusion
and without despair'.[24]

An important exception which throws into question the
general criticism of neo-orthodoxy is to be found in the Committee of Southern Churchmen to which reference has been
made earlier. It was organized in 1964 to draw together in in-
formal structure the clergy and laymen in the south who believe
that the problem of the Church in dealing with race relations
is basically a theological one. The staff person for the Committee
stated this position in the first issue of the journal published
by the Committee:

> The Church has failed in the matter of race because we have
> called it 'social action' when all the while it was evangelism.
> . . . Repeatedly those of us who attend social action conferences
> hear it lamented that the Church has 'lost its mission'. The speaker
> generally infers that the *mission* of the Church is social action. He
> does not seem to realize that his Division of Social Action was prob-
> ably created by the Establishment to avoid evangelism and thus to
> avoid social action – an evangelism that sees all of life as incarna-
> tional; a social action that follows as naturally as breathing.[25]

This group has been actively involved in the desegregation
process in the southern states while firmly maintaining that the
humanist approach is – for the church – a dead-end street. It
stresses that it is God's reconciliation of men to himself through
Christ which requires and enables the faith and lives of Christians to reflect the *fact* of reconciliation. The tenacity of the

24 Reinhold Niebuhr, 'The Quality of our Lives', *The Christian Century*, Vol.
LXXVII, No. 19, May 11, 1960, p. 571.
25 Will D. Campbell, *Katallagete*, Vol. I, No. 1, June 1965, p. 5.

group and its ability to relate to the prejudiced and to the victims of prejudice gives rise to the speculation that what Protestantism in the United States labelled as a theology of despair (and therefore rejected) might have had important contributions to make in the racial crisis.

Relational Theology

Relational theology arose both as a reaction against neo-orthodoxy and as a response to the increasing depersonalization of American society. By the end of the 1950's several writers were speaking of the marked decline in theological creativity in American Protestantism, and much of the blame for this was placed on the central position which neo-orthodoxy had occupied. Critics contended that its use of traditional language had inhibited the development of newer theological ideas and that its emphasis on the Church had been unproductive – ('. . . a self-conscious centring on the church is a kind of religious narcissism that destroys spontaneity.')[26] Various suggestions were offered as an antidote for the supposed sterility. The major emphasis in these was on the personal. As one writer stated it, 'It is the unique responsibility and opportunity of Protestantism today to encourage the individual in his personal existence and search, to help sharpen the issues of his life and to insist that he take the time to be and become himself.'[27] Another critic wrote:

Beyond the formal technical knowledge of man, beyond the externals of communication, beyond the things that are the coin of civilization, the manipulables of the clever, the arbiters of power, beyond all these, is the inner sanctuary of the self, the true person. This sanctuary is the final citadel of life. It is the contact point with God and with man. It is that which abides when all else is taken from us. Here we minister to one another, are priests to one another, and stand together with all men against that which would destroy us. Here the machine, the apparatus, was conceived. Here it must be conquered.[28]

[26] Warren Ashby, 'The Task of Protestantism Today', *The Christian Century*, Vol. LXXVII, No. 43, October 25, 1961, p. 1269.

[27] *Ibid.*, pp. 1270-1271.

[28] Edward V. Stein, 'Persons in a Depersonalized Age', *The Christian Century*, Vol. LXXVII, No. 25, June 22, 1960, p. 746.

Relational theology emerged as the result of such concerns and diagnoses. It received intellectual sustenance from the theology of Martin Buber and the philosophy of personalism. Its emphasis on the importance of interpersonal relationships and dialogue made it particularly attractive to American laymen with their bias towards 'need-filling' theology. One of the more influential interpreters of relational theology is Reuel Howe, author of *Man's Need and God's Action*, which has been used extensively across the Protestant churches as a basis for discussion groups. In the foreword to the book Canon Theodore Wedel states the case for this theological emphasis:

> The presentation of the Christian Gospel, traditionally familiar to us, normally takes the form of proclamation . . . The Gospel, in other words, begins with God and not with man. In an age of increasing religious illiteracy, however, proclamation of the Gospel requires prepared minds and hearts . . . The 'language of Canaan' . . . must be made relevant to life as modern men and women know it. Verbal presentations of the Gospel frequently find themselves giving answers to questions that have not been asked – or not asked as yet.
>
> Can there, accordingly, be an approach to the Gospel which begins at the other end? Can we start with questions and not with answers? Can we lead modern men and women to face the mystery of themselves and their deeper hungers for salvation, often unacknowledged, for which the Gospel can then become light and healing? This pedagogic procedure looks dangerous at first . . . yet the method of correlating question and answer, human need and revelation, if tried in faith, may lead to astonishing results. Dialogue replaces monologue.[29]

Two leaders of the Negro religious community base their theology on a relational or person-centred theological emphasis. George Kelsey, professor of Christian Ethics at the Theological School of Drew University, has used Buber's 'I-Thou' philosophy in a creative and challenging explanation of racism. His thesis is that racism in its modern manifestations is a faith, a particularly pernicious form of idolatry. As he explains it, the racist consciousness operates in 'the world of It'. The 'I' self does not enter into communion with the other, for the other is not known

---

[29] Reuel I. Howe, *Man's Need and God's Action* (New York, The Seabury Press, 1953), pp. vii-viii.

as 'Thou'. The other always remains an 'It', but the consciousness which alienates and dominates makes itself a correlate of
that which it enslaves. In the context of race relations, the racist
lives entirely in the 'I-It' world, and he can never find himself
in this world as a person, for to live alone in the 'I-It' world
is not to be a 'real man'.[30] It is difficult to gauge the extent of
Kelsey's influence, but a large number of young Negro ministers
have been exposed to his theology.

Martin Luther King attended the Boston University School of
Theology, which has been dominated by a personalist philosophy throughout this century. There is no question concerning
the extent of King's influence on the Negro community. Some
persons, however, have questioned whether his theological
influence has been a beneficial one. One theologian who is a
Negro has said that King's attempt to combine love and the
strategy of non-violence is a theological failure – that he has
borrowed the syncretic spirit of Gandhi, 'and it is as though
Socrates, Thoreau, Hegel, and Jesus were all dumped together
into one philosophical bowl like tossed salad' and that 'It is this
syncretistic inclination combined with King's undoubted impact
that continues to make Negroes mistake religion for faith.'[31]
Another of King's critics contends that because of his theology
the non-violent movement has operated with an ethic which is
an inversion of contemporary ethics, that its leaders have insis-
ted that love is more relevant than justice in reforming society,
and that justice seems to stand as the highest good of a Christian society with love being the method of this goal. The truth
is probably that King's theological influence has been very
slight, but that his personal impact has been considerably
strengthened by the fact that his own life seems to be an em-
bodiment of his theology.

An assessment of the influence which relational theology may
have had on the Protestantism of the United States is difficult
because unlike neo-orthodoxy it does not seem to have reached
its crest yet, and it is of such a nature that it can be assimilated

[30] George D. Kelsey, *Racism and the Christian Understanding of Man* (New
York, Charles Scribner's Sons, 1965), *passim*.
[31] Joseph R. Washington, Jr., *Black Religion* (Boston, Beacon Press, 1964),
p. 8.

quite easily by the prevailing Puritanism-revivalism-Social
Gospel theology. One could not anticipate its offering anything
radically new to the race relations ethic of a Protestantism
which has generally been dominated by man-centred theology.

Radical Christianity

The latest development on the American theological scene is a
much-expanded version of the English 'God is dead' school. In
the United States the name most often used to designate this
theological emphasis is radical Christianity. There is a wide
diversity of belief among the theologians associated with this
trend – enough so that some of them classify themselves
as either 'hard' or 'soft' radicals – but much more of what one
might call a school emerged than in the case of any other theological emphasis in the contemporary situation. A perusal of
theological journals of the 1960's shows increasing attention and
space being devoted to articles by men identified with this theology, and one secular magazine, *The New Yorker*, devoted three
issues to an investigation of it in 1965. Some of the theologians
who are considered representative of this attempted radical reconstruction of theology are William Hamilton, Paul van
Buren, Langdon Gilkey, Schubert Ogden, Harvey Cox, and
Thomas Altizer. While differing on specifics, they would probably agree with Gilkey's characterization of the school as being
composed of those men who say, 'Let us . . . cease to talk about
God, or the divine, for the universe around is absurd and only
the void is real. And let us speak only of the figure of Jesus and
his call to love.'[32]

Gilkey attributes the move towards a 'new' theology to the
fact that there was a 'steady dissolution' of all the certainties
which had bolstered neo-orthodox theology in the United
States during the 1950's. This dissolution he sees as being a result
of the inability of that theology to communicate with modern
man and as a result of the increasingly potent mood of secularism in the United States. In spite of the fact that radical Chris-

---

[32] Langdon Gilkey, 'Dissolution and Reconstruction in Theology', *The
Christian Century*, Vol. LXXXII, No. 5, February 3, 1965, p. 136.

tianity is a revolt against older theology, it acknowledges its indebtedness to neo-orthodoxy from which it has mainly drawn negative implications. Paul Tillich with his emphasis on relevance and communication was probably the spiritual father of this movement in the United States even though he is criticized for not having carried his emphasis far enough. Undoubtedly, however, the writings of Dietrich Bonhoeffer have been the greatest single influence on this group of American theologians. Bonhoeffer's phrase 'a world come of age' has become a normative, descriptive term in United States Protestantism in much the same manner that Buber's 'I-Thou' terminology has been accepted. Many serious students of Bonhoeffer question whether radical theologians have really wrestled as they should with the corpus of Bonhoeffer's work. For example, it is difficult to see how Hamilton can speak seriously of Bonhoeffer's 'vision of a theology without a doctrine of God, a doctrine of the church or eschatology'.[33] However, while there is room for dispute about interpretation, it is from Bonhoeffer that the terminology and seed ideas of the 'new' theology have been borrowed.

In spite of the diversity of thought among the radical theologians, there seem to be three shared points of concern. All are concerned in some way with an interpretation of the reality behind the phrase 'death of God'. These range from the belief that man's traditional religious idea of God is dead, in that it is no longer relevant to a secular age, to the belief that the metaphor expresses the truth that ours is a history in which God is no longer present. The second point of concern is with Christology, and this is a somewhat natural outcome of the first. It is obvious that a 'Godless' Christology presents problems. The general trend of radical theology is away from Christology towards 'Jesusology' with an emphasis on an ethic based on the life of Jesus. 'The Christian is defined, therefore, as the man bound to Jesus, obedient to him and obedient as he was obedient.'[34] And finally, radical Christianity produces an essentially 'optimistic' theology. A doctrine of sin is only of peri-

[33] William Hamilton, 'A Secular Theology for a World Come of Age', *Theology Today*, Vol. 18, January 1962, p. 458.
[34] William Hamilton, 'The Shape of a Radical Theology', *The Christian Century*, Vol. LXXXII, No. 40, October 6, 1965, p. 1221.

pheral importance. This theology is optimistic about man's possibilities and abilities, and its attitude towards the world and culture is one of affirmation. Hamilton says, 'This optimism is found in today's Negro revolution, and the radical theology wishes to learn from and respond to this decisive movement in our natural life.'[35]

One cannot yet determine if there has been any relationship between radical theology and the Negro revolution. Its focus on man and his culture which produces an ethic of identification would not be at cross purposes with the ideology of the civil rights movement. The basic questions, however, are what contribution it would have to make which is in any way different from any other sociological analysis, and whether a doctrine of man derived in this way throws any essential new light on man's humanity. The most vocal critics of radical theology contend that it is neither radical nor new – that it is indeed the Social Gospel dressed in the vocabulary of the mid-20th century.

This quite brief examination of the new trends in the theology of American Protestantism suggests that anthropocentricism continues to be the distinguishing mark of American theology. Dialectical theology with its emphasis on a doctrine of sin and neo-orthodoxy with its emphasis on Christology and a doctrine of the Church exercised at best a slight tempering influence. The Protestant community in the United States continues to search for an understanding of itself and its relationship to the world with its eyes fixed steadfastly on 20th century man and 20th century America.

[35] *Ibid.*

A THEOLOGICAL POSTSCRIPT

That is it – the ugly history of race relations in the United States and the not very noble role that Protestantism has played in this history. The question which provoked this study was whether the theology of American Protestantism has been to any extent responsible for its record. My study has convinced me that this is so, but in this condensation of it I have only tried to indicate that the theology of Protestantism has at least allowed for the impotence of the churches. Its anthropocentricism which has led to a theology of a dead God, a gentle Jesus, and a fellowship of believers in the deity of man, has also led to an ethical failure which is neither surprising nor shocking. Both the action and the inaction of the churches are reasonable consequences of their interpretation of doctrines and/or the precedence which has been given to certain doctrines. It would perhaps be better to leave it here, but, of course, one cannot. If the anthropocentricism of American theology has allowed for ethical impotence, wherein lies the possibility of potence? This is what I wish to explore now. I am convinced more strongly each day that the colour problem is not confined to those areas of the world like the United States, South Africa, or Rhodesia where one sees it in its most blatant and notorious forms. The daily papers announce that the problems engendered by the colours of our skins are worldwide. No one of us is likely to escape the necessity of dealing for ourselves with the meaning of our whiteness or blackness.

1

Anthropocentric Theology

To summarize: The covenant theology of New England Puritanism was an elaborate causistry designed to justify the ways of an implacable God to man. Its interpretation of covenant as contract implied that God was controlled by man. Man and his salvation became more and more the focus of that theology. Revivalism's chief concern was man's salvation which he achieved by repentance as attested to by a conversion experience. Thus, God's grace was conditioned by man's action. The Social Gospel movement was avowedly anthropocentric. It understood man's salvation in a social context and as being involved with the re-ordering of society. God's grace was in that instance conditioned by economic and sociological realities. Dialectical theology was unable to move from man in society to man in the community of the Church. The first concern of relational theology is man's need which the Scriptures indicate is God's concern, but the Scriptures indicate that man is not able rightly to comprehend his need until he has heard the Word. Radical theology is man's abandonment of the God he cannot control.

The theology of American Protestantism has consistently fallen into the error of allowing a separation of or confusion between the divine and human nature of Christ and a separation between his person and work. The historical tendency to concentrate on the humanity of Christ has allowed an anthropological approach to theology which has made man both the subject and object of theological enquiry. As we have seen, the doctrines of God, of Christ, and of the Church have been shaped and moulded by man's understanding of himself in terms of his society and his needs.

Two generalizations can be made in summarizing the witness of American Protestantism in the area of race relations. First, there has been no period in American history when there have not been voices from within the churches raised in protest against racial injustice. These have often been lonely voices, but in the early anti-slavery movement, the non-violence movement of the 1950's, and between 1963 and 1966, sizable segments of the churches have been involved. In the second place, the action of the churches has assumed something of the nature of a crusade rather than being an integral part of the life and witness of the Church. The activism which one might expect from a man-centred theology is pervasive in American churches, but it is of a limited and sporadic nature. Race relations has been seen (if at all) as one among a number of ethical problems with which the churches must deal rather than as a theological issue. It is for this reason that the churches could plan three-year 'crash' programmes and delegate large budgets to these and then turn their attention elsewhere. It is for this reason that the churches were able to convince themselves in 1967 that it was appropriate to concentrate on the War on Poverty programme which had a direct relationship to the problems of Negroes but which did not require separate committees and budgets as had the 'crash' programmes on race relations. It is because race relations has been considered an ethical problem that the 'white churches' and white Christians are so easily discouraged by their inability to solve the problem and are so easily led into indifference or cynicism.

Christocentric Theology

Christian theology is Christocentric theology. This is not to say that all theology can be reduced to Christology, but it is to insist that it is Jesus Christ to whom the Christians must look to see the truth about God, man, and the world. All doctrines must be formulated and expressed in the light of God's revelation in Jesus Christ.

It is not only the content of theology which is informed by its Christological centre, but the starting point of theology is determined by God's revelation of himself. In Jesus Christ the initiative has been assumed by God. God has entered the world and has met man on his home ground. Man need not search for an absent or hidden God – he has come amongst us. In his own freedom God has chosen to tabernacle with man. He has done so not because of man's importunity nor because of man's merit or works; he has come to man who could not go to him because it is his good pleasure to reveal himself to man and to be reconciled to him. In Jesus Christ it is made perfectly clear that the primary movement of the Christian faith is the movement of God to man. Therefore, theology must choose as its starting point Jesus Christ, for it is in him that God has chosen to meet man.

Jesus Christ, God-man

In Jesus Christ the impregnable barrier between God and man has been breached. In him God encounters man, and in him man encounters God. He is very God and very man. As we look at Jesus Christ, we see the face of God – God who wills to show himself to man, to humble himself, to suffer death at the hands of man in order that reconciliation may be effected. God gives that which he alone can give – himself. We see the God whose love is judgment and whose judgment is mercy. As we look at Jesus Christ, we see the face of man. He is the prototype of all men, and it is through him that we understand true humanity. Man is no longer a struggling creature who must propitiate an angry God. Manhood and sonship are given to man in Jesus Christ. In him we are restored to our true condition as sons of God.

Jesus Christ is the Covenant between God and man. He is Mediator at both poles of the Covenant: God for us, and we with God. In Jesus Christ we see enacted the whole history of God and man – the establishment of covenant, its rupture, and its re-establishment. In Jesus Christ God and man live through together the drama of history from perfection to fall to redemption. Jesus, the perfect one, elects to become the cursed and bear in his own body the sin of man. He stands in man's place and is condemned to death and separation from God. This is the condition of man when the Covenant has been negated. It is we who have negated the Covenant. Our attitude towards God is not one of indifference or carelessness; we desire to reign in his place. We desire this so strongly as to have become murderers of his son. But God's final word in Jesus Christ is the word of resurrection, of victory over death, of re-establishment of the Covenant. The risen Christ is the New Man in whom the Covenant is reconstituted for all humanity.

In Jesus Christ the Covenant is concluded. His history is the history of man, his death the death of man, his resurrection the restoration of man. We think now in terms of an accomplished victory and an effected reconciliation. Jesus Christ is not our assistant; he is our righteousness and our sanctification. The charges which should have been laid against us have been laid against him. He has been declared guilty and condemned to death in our place. He has satisfied the judgment of God and in his resurrection has triumphed over chastisement. We now see that the judgment of God is synonomous with his love; he judges in order to save.

Man who could not become righteous by obedience to the Law was made righteous through the obedience of God's Son. Man's righteousness is imputed to him. The Old Testament is the record of man's inability to fulfil the Law – to live in conformity to the will of God. The Gospel declares this impossible and unnecessary – what we cannot do for ourselves has been done for us. We are restored to a right relationship with God through Jesus Christ who is the righteousness of the unrighteous.

The same Jesus Christ who is our righteousness is our sanctification. Santification is neither obedience to precepts nor the sum of human virtues. Sanctification is the exaltation of man in Jesus Christ; it is the creation of man's new form of existence as the faithful Covenant partner of God. Because we are new beings, our acts express the new life which is in us. We act in gratitude for what has been done for us, but we act in a new way because we cannot do otherwise. Our acts agree with the work of God in Christ which is the work which fashions us. But it is not our obedience which sanctifies us; it is the obedience of Jesus Christ which makes the justification and sanctification of man secure into eternity.

The Church

God has called all men into Covenant relationship with himself through his calling of Jesus Christ. In him God has willed to set man in community. The new relationship between God and man and among men centres in the Church. It is Christ who fashions, bears, and protects the Church. It has no perfection or truth of its own; it only bears signs of the perfection or truth of Christ. It points always away from itself to Another. If the Church tries to find its life in itself, it ceases to be the Body of Christ and becomes a social or religious body. If the Church knows its life to be in Christ and his presence therein continually leads it to repentance and renewed life, it is the Body of Christ. Its imperfections do not count against it for it abides in Christ not because of its merits but by the grace of God. It is already presented in its purity by Christ to the Father.

The Church is assembled and made manifest in the world by the work of the Holy Spirit. The Spirit is present and active where the name of Christ is spoken and heard, and it is he who acts to accomplish among men what has been accomplished in Jesus Christ – a communion, reconciliation, the Church. The Holy Spirit associates us with Christ and establishes between him and us, and among all men, the bond of peace. It is he who leads the Church away from itself and along the path of life, death, and resurrection of its Lord. Thus, he establishes the pattern of life of the Church.

The Church and the World

The relationship between the Church and the world has been established and revealed by God's action in Jesus Christ. The Church is often unable to see this relationship clearly.

On the one hand, the Church is tempted to set itself apart from the world. It is tempted to see itself as a holy people or a holy place in a world of evil. It becomes fearful for its purity and holiness; it walls itself away behind its goodness; it clutches its truth to itself in order that it be not contaminated by the world's falsehoods. This is to forget that it has no purity, holiness, goodness, or truth of its own. The Church does not possess these attributes in opposition to an evil world; the Church is possessed by the One who is purity, holiness, goodness, and truth. When the Church looks away from this One to itself, when it fails to see its oneness with the world in sin and redemption, when it separates itself from the world, it separates itself from Jesus Christ.

On the other hand, the Church is tempted to lose itself in the world. When the Church becomes obsessed with the world to the point that it speaks and acts as though God's obsession with the world awaits its consummation in a work of the Church, it is usurping to itself the work of redemption. When the Church believes it can and should meet the world outside of Jesus Christ, that it must cloak its message in forms which are familiar or acceptable to the world, that the world can be beguiled, flattered or hoodwinked into becoming the Church, then it shares the world's blindness. The Church which is over-anxious for the world comes to idolize the world and forgoes its rightful place in the world.

These two temptations of the Church are two aspects of the failure to realize that the unity which God has established in Christ means that the Church and world are neither identified with each other nor isolated from each other. The will of God for the Church is his will for the world, but the Church and the world exist in tension. The Church's proclamation of God's love for the world calls the world into question and forces it to see itself under God's judgment. But the Word of the Church to the world is Jesus Christ who is forgiveness and in whom reconciliation has been accomplished. The provisional tension which exists between the Church and the world is acknowledged and occasioned only indirectly by the Church as it proclaims the One in whom all tension has been resolved.

The Christian Ethic

The point of departure for the Christian ethic is the reconciliation which has been wrought in Jesus Christ, which is to say that the Christian ethic is centred in the Church. This is because God's will for the Church and the world is the same; he wills and achieves reconciliation. The reconciliation between God and man which has been effected in Jesus Christ for all men is actualized in his Body, the community of believers, through the power of his Spirit.

Because God establishes man in community there is no individual ethic for the Christian. Man's individuality, his personhood, his freedom is found in relationship with his fellow men. By the very fact that Jesus Christ has stood for man before God

and has acted in his place, by the very nature of the reconciliation which has been effected, the Christian stands and acts
always in the great company of the reconciled. My 'I' is 'I' only
in the 'we' in which I have been placed in Jesus Christ. I have
been placed among those who acknowledge Jesus Christ as Lord
for the sake of those who do not yet know his Lordship. God
is *pro me* only because he is *pro nobis*.

The Christian ethic is concerned with the responsibility of the
Church for the world. Its sum and substance is the proclamation
of Jesus Christ. But just as the word and act of God are one
in Jesus Christ, there is no separation between the word and
act of the Church. If the Church speaks the word which it is
not, it is impotent; it becomes one of the many voices which
harangue the world. If the word of the Church is proclamation
– the spreading abroad of the good news – this word is self-
authenticating and efficacious.

The Church has no programme to offer to set the world
right; it has instead the startling message that the world has
been set right. What the Church says to the world is that despite
all seemingly contradictory evidence the problem of morality
has been resolved. God has taken upon himself the solution.
Jesus Christ has lived out the response of man to God which
is in conformity to God's will for the world. Man's concern is
with the reception of this response as the response for him and
all men, and he is enabled by God so to receive it. Therefore,
the word of the Church to the world is always Gospel. The
Church has no word of judgment or condemnation to speak to
the world. The judgment and condemnation of both the Church
and the world have been satisfied by the death of Jesus Christ.
There is no exception. The world is not capable of any atrocity
so heinous that the Church is allowed to speak to it any word
other than the Word of God: Jesus Christ.

The response of the Christian to every human problem is the
witness that God in his being and action among us has himself
become the solution of human problems. The Christian community witnesses to the fact that man has been freed from
himself to become the Covenant partner of God. His life, therefore, is one of fully human, active, responsible participation

in the world. Man need not use an imagined freedom as a pretext to play God. Man is free to be what he is enabled to be – true man; he is freed from the burden of being what he cannot be – God. The freedom which God has ordained for man in Christ is primarily freedom *for* life. It is the freedom for love which makes the Christian unfree for hatred; it is the freedom for a re-conciled life which makes a life of schism an impossible option for the Christian. The positive nature of this freedom produces the characteristic note of the life of the Church which is joy.

Theology, the Christian Community, and Race Relations

There is much to be learned from a study of history, but what is learned evokes from the Christian community confession rather than criticism. The final 'yes' or 'no' concerning the faith-fulness of God's people remains with God. The question which the past presents to the present is whether the churches are the Church; whether their lives reflect the life, death, and resur-rection of Christ; whether their word to the world is the Word. The answer to this question is a confession of the present oppor-tunity and task which is given to the Church by its Lord.

The Christian community is enabled to see that the broken-ness of man's relationships is a manifestation of his inhuman condition when he is outside the Covenant relationship or when he has forgotten or disavowed the Covenant. For this reason, all programmes aimed at overcoming this inhuman condition must be seen as problematic and of an extremely tentative nature. The Church is concerned for justice and with all pos-sibilities for the re-ordering of society which will enable men to live in more amicable and equitable relationships. But the Christian understands too well the depth of man's alienation from man to place ultimate confidence in any humanly-contrived solution for the overcoming of this alienation. Therefore, the *primary* witness of the Christian community in a world torn asunder by racial hostility and conflict cannot be a crusade against segregation or the presentation of a blueprint for an integrated society. The witness of the Church is to an achieved reconciliation which lies beyond human possibility.

The Church is the community of those who have suffered reconciliation; it is also the community of those who are at all times suffering anew their reconciliation. Its peace and wholeness lie not in itself but in Jesus Christ who is its Lord. The Church does not point to itself as the example, source, or hope of reconciliation. In the face of its own brokenness the Church can only turn to the Source of wholeness and offer itself in repentance. If its voicing of repentance is mere preamble to its own plans for healing itself or the world, there will be no healing. It is only as the Church understands its reconciliation as a gift and the continuing activity of God that it is able to proclaim reconciliation to the yet unreconciled.

The witness of the Church in this time of racial conflict can be considered by speaking of four words – proclaiming, listening, standing and interceding. These words do not describe separable activities to which an order of precedence can be given, nor are they uniquely related to a time of crisis. They are descriptive of the style of life which is appropriate to the Christian community at any time.

The proclamation of the Church is not altered by the situation in which it is made. This is so because its message is not its own but is given to it; this message is sufficient for the wrath and hostility of the world which may vary from time to time in degree but not in nature. The word of the Church is direct, unequivocal, particular, and precise. It is this because it is a recapitulation of the Word of God and his action which always bear these characteristics. The word of the Church to the world of racial hostility both within and without itself is: Be ye reconciled. As imperative it is spoken in conjunction with the indicative: Ye are reconciled. The call to reconciliation which is entrusted to Christians as ambassadors of Christ is a possibility only because reconciliation has been accomplished. The Christian stands in the place where racial hostility has erupted into violence, and even dies there, in the sure knowledge that hostility and violence is not the truth about the world. The patience and persistence with which the Church proclaims reconciliation is unending, for it does so in the steadfast knowledge that Christ is at work in the world.

The Church must listen to and hear the word of the world. This is not because the message of the Church to the world is determined by the world's demands upon the Church, but because Christ may choose to minister to the Church through the voices of those who do not yet acknowledge him as Lord. The Church may offer words of advice to governments and lawmakers, financial assistance to the poor and oppressed, and programmes and palliatives to the exploited – only to discover that the demands of the world are far more exorbitant. The world may have asked the Church to stand with it in its poverty and blindness; it may have asked the Church not for a dole but for its life. The Church listens to the world in the constant expectation of this demand for a freedom and love which are beyond human possibility – and the inability of the world to make articulate its need is a constant reminder to the Church of its own inability to make articulate its plenitude – which is Jesus Christ.

The Church and the world stand *together* in the face of the onslaught of sin and death which manifests itself in racial hatred. The Church does not stand *by* the world as though impervious to this power of death; it knows that it has fallen victim to hatred, that it has allowed itself to be torn, shattered, rendered impotent, and controlled by racism. The world does not see the issue as having to do with the power of sin and death at work in the world. The world sees the issues of racial conflict as being those of segregation and integration, weakness and power, injustice and justice, oppression and freedom. The Church recognizes these as valid but partial understandings. Christians are to be found on picket lines, in protest marches, at black power conferences – wherever attempts are being made to establish conditions in which people can live more fully. But Christians are there as a response to the work of Christ in making the world human rather than in adherence to rigid programmes or philosophies. The world may reject the Church because its stand for justice cannot become a stand against an enemy. The Christian has no choice but to love the one who seems to stand against him. This means that the Christian does not cease to love the ones who persecute him. This means quite specifically that the ministry of the Church is to the perpetrators of hatred and violence (e.g. segregationists, the Ku Klux Klan, the John Birch Society, the Black Muslims, the rioting Negro mobs) exactly as it is to those who suffer violence and hatred. Reconciliation requires and enables the loving of one's neighbour though he appear in the guise of one's enemy.

The stand of the Church is not predicated on the basis of success. The Christian does not eschew competence, skill, or effectiveness; his actions may demonstrate all of these qualities. But the Christian knows that Christ's reconciliation of men is neither social stratagem nor political expedient but is the gift of God. He knows, too, that this gift involves the Cross, and that the time may be (and may have been) at hand when acceptance of the Cross is the only witness open to white or black men. This witness appears always inefficient and insufficient to the world; it is other than this in the economy of God.

The final word which describes the witness of the Church in racial conflict is intercession. In its intercessory prayer the Church presents itself wholly to the Father of its Lord and offers itself as representative of the world on behalf of the world. This work of the Church mirrors the work of God in Christ by which man's reconciliation was accomplished; and it is, therefore, the authentic witness which the Church is commanded and permitted to make to the world. The world (and the churches) may question the efficacy of this witness; the Church it not allowed nor tempted to do so.

The witness of the Church at all times and in all places is a witness to the reconciliation which has been consummated for all men by the action of God in Jesus Christ. The dividing wall of hostility has been broken down, and all of us who were afar have been brought near. We have been made one in Jesus Christ. The ultimate fact of our existence is neither that we are black nor white, nor slave nor free; we are the sons of God. The Church witnesses to this fact with the totality of its life in the sure knowledge that neither colour, nor 'death, nor life, nor angels, nor principalities, nor things present, nor things to come, nor powers, nor height, nor depth, nor anything in all creation, will be able to separate us from the love of God in Christ Jesus our Lord'.

INDEX

Printed in Great Britain
at Hopetoun Street, Edinburgh,
by T. and A. CONSTABLE LTD.
Printers to the University of Edinburgh